THE SHOOTING SCRIPT™

DEAD MAN WALKING

DEAD MAN WALKING

INTRODUCTION, SCREENPLAY, AND NOTES BY
TIM ROBBINS

FOREWORD BY
SISTER HELEN PREJEAN

A Newmarket Shooting Script™ Series Book
NEWMARKET PRESS • NEW YORK

First Edition

97 98 99   10 9 8 7 6 5 4 3 2 1

Library of Congress Cataloging-in-Publication Data

Robbins, Tim, 1958–
Dead man walking : the shooting script / screenplay, introduction, and notes by Tim Robbins ;
based on the book Dead man walking by Sister Helen Prejean.
p.   cm.   — (A Newmarket shooting script series book)
ISBN 1-55704-300-0
I. Dead man walking (Motion picture)   II. Prejean, Helen. Dead man walking.   III. Title.   IV. Series.
PN1997.D375   1996

791.43'72—dc21   96-47471
                                                                                                      CIP

Quantity Purchases

Companies, professional groups, clubs, and other organizations may qualify for special terms
when ordering quantities of this title. For information, write Special Sales, Newmarket Press,
18 East 48th Street, New York, NY 10017, call (212) 832-3575, or fax (212) 832-3629.

Book design by Tania Garcia
Manufactured in the United States of America

OTHER NEWMARKET MOVIEBOOKS INCLUDE

CONTENTS

INTRODUCTION

BY TIM ROBBINS

I remember seeing action/adventure movies as a child. Our hero pursues a villain who has committed a terrible crime, killed the one the hero loved. In the final reel of the picture our hero stands over the beaten villain, gun in hand, raises the gun, aims at the villain's head. Silence. The villain breathes heavily, desperately. Close up on hero as he speaks. "No, I'm not going to kill you." He puts the gun down, disgust on his face. The police arrive. Wow, I thought. Why didn't he shoot him? I would have. The answer didn't find its way to me until later. He didn't kill him because it is immoral, it is illegal, and because he is a hero. In a moment of passion our hero would not kill. He would not take the understandable step of avenging his loved one's death. He did not sink to vengeance. He took the high ground, he became an enigma, a mysterious superhuman.

In today's action/adventure, the hero has the gun pointed at the villain's head in the final reel. The hero says something clever, which usually gets a laugh; he presses the trigger, shoots the villain between the eyes, blood splatters, and the audience applauds, hoots, and hollers.

While I was editing *Dead Man Walking* I thought a lot about this scenario. I replayed that scene over and over in my head. Finally I realized why. These action/adventure movies, having conceded vengeance to their heroes, had become strangely moral-less, pro-death penalty films. Our hero acts as judge, jury, and executioner. This is instant justice, vigilantism with no consequence. What had happened? How had we become so jaded? Had nihilism won? Were there no heroes because we had given up believing in them, or did we not have enough faith in ourselves as writers, directors, and actors to create plausible heroic characters who would not stoop to revenge? Were we all so frustrated with the crime around us that we needed to see evil die again and again?

When we began to shoot *Dead Man Walking* in April 1995 in New Orleans, Louisiana, all expectations of its commercial appeal were very low. We're doing a little movie, I would say. Certainly no one was being paid much. I warned Sister Helen Prejean, the author of the book on which the movie was based, not to have high expectations. We're doing a record of a time, I would say; people may not see it when it comes out, but they will see it as time passes. For me successful movies work ten years from now. Little did anyone know of the rocket that would take off when the film was released. As I write this the film is on a pace to make $90 million worldwide. Having been in films that have not reached that level with frightening regularity, I am slow to attach any importance or significance to this number. I mention it now as a way of saying that somewhere close to 20 million people have seen this movie.

Why do people go to this movie? I really don't know. There are stunning performances, the story is gripping, the camera work excellent. But I have seen films with these elements that have failed to bring in people. What is it about Sister Helen's story that has captured the public unconscious, that has tapped into the mysterious and elusive zeitgeist?

A month after the film came out, I received a letter from a prison guard in Wisconsin who recounted a memory of a very quiet inmate, in for murder, who came to him with excitement in his eyes one day. He took the guard outside to show him some flowers he had planted, pride overwhelming him. That got this guard thinking about the difference between him and the inmate. What was it that led him to his crime? "Never was loved," was his simple answer. "How desperately we all need love," he wrote.

Early on in filming, Susan Sarandon saw the film as a love story. She was right on target. The film we were doing, while centered around the impending execution of Matt Poncelet, had at its heart something entirely different. It was about love—true love— courageous, independent, unconditional love. How many of us ever find unconditional love? Some are lucky enough as children to receive it from parents, but after that where do we find it? In our lives we pay for our mistakes, whether in prison for crimes against society or in our homes for infidelities, rudeness, deeply wounding comments. Years can pass before forgiveness, and some can never find it in their hearts to love unconditionally, continually hanging on to the other's past indiscretions to wield power in their homes.

Reading Sister Helen's book and seeing Sean's and Susan's performances evolve, one was confronted with an unsettling paradox, the ultimate challenge laid down by Jesus, "Love your enemy." Certainly an unpopular sentiment in this country. As a culture, we embrace conflict. We love seeing couples split up, yelling at each other on talk shows. We tolerate trash talk between athletes. We cheer when the villain dies in our movie theaters. We demonize our enemies and fight wars to defeat evil. But forgiveness? Compassion? Understanding? We honor these traits, we revere them, but we reserve them as special, something only the truly enlightened, the saintly can achieve. In the book *Dead Man Walking,* and in the movie, we are presented with a nun, imperfect and unprepared, just like you and me, who is challenged to live up to her faith and love her enemy. She somehow finds the strength to do so, reconciling his sins and praying for his redemption. In the final moments of the film we, too, grieve for a fallen soul; we, too, feel compassion for the parents of the victims, and we, too, abhor violence of all kinds. We accept Helen's unconditional love as a viable attainable thing, as a strength, not a weakness. Perhaps this is why so many people found their way to this film. Perhaps there is a need to believe that in the final reel of a movie we do not have to lower ourselves by cheering for retribution. We can show strength with a resolute love, an uncompromising moral compass. We, too, can love unconditionally. We can be the hero, put down our gun and say, I will not kill.

FOREWORD

BY SISTER HELEN PREJEAN

I t's been amazing to watch the screenplay develop, seeing how Tim Robbins fashioned scenes and characters and dialogue from my book, *Dead Man Walking*. I was right in there with him on every line, every scene; that's part of his creative genius, that he's not tight and rigid and ego-controlled, so he could let me and others collaborate with him in shaping the story.

His great challenge was to make a riveting film about a nun and a death-row inmate, which did not include some kind of hanky-panky between them or her helping him escape or sneaking a cyanide pill into the death house so he could take himself out like Socrates. Or—surprise—he's really innocent, and she gets the truth known just before they kill him and saves his life. Tim would have none of that, which is why I knew I could trust him to make a film of my book.

From the beginning Tim seemed sure about a few core things: that the crime would be truthfully portrayed; that the death-row inmate, Matthew Poncelet, would be guilty as sin and repulsive; that the suffering of the victims' families would be sympathetically rendered; that I, the nun, would not be portrayed as a plaster saint who didn't make any mistakes ("Saints are boring"); that the film would be art, not a polemic against the death penalty; and that lethal injection would replace the electric chair ("We need to explore if there is a truly humane way to kill a human being").

Crafting the screenplay presented daunting challenges. Where's the drama in scene after scene of a nun and a convict talking to each other with bare walls around them, physically separated by bars or mesh screen? It's the ultimate nightmare of filmmakers: talking heads. And where would the conflict be, the climax of the story?

"That hymn, 'Be not afraid,' did you sing to the inmate in the death house?" Tim asks.

"No, I played a tape."

"I think we'll have Susan sing it."

"Oh, she sings well?"

"I think she does. But she's terrified. (laughing) It will make it more poignant." So Susan Sarandon's singing part in the film was born.

One scene that came into the film late was the speeding scene when a state trooper stops me and says, "I never gave a ticket to no nun before. Hmmmm. (big pause) Gave a ticket to an IRS agent one time and got audited that year." In real life this happened to me four days after we started filming in New Orleans. I told Tim about it, and he said, "He said that about the IRS? Write down everything you remember and fax it over to me." They shot the speeding scene the next Wednesday, setting a record, I'll bet, for the quickest turnover from real life to celluloid that's ever taken place.

I teased Tim about getting the nuns right. After all, he went to a Catholic school and was taught by nuns. In his first draft he had me putting the habit back on because the prison chaplain told me to. "No way," I wrote in the margin. We haven't worn the habit for twenty years, and I surely wouldn't put it on because some chaplain told me to.

Tim had his stubborn side. In the scene when Poncelet is eating his last meal, he holds up a fried shrimp and says how good it is and that he had never eaten shrimp. In the margins I wrote: "Somebody from Louisiana who never had shrimp? Unbelievable." Then I'm on the set, we're about to shoot the last meal, and I object again about Poncelet's unfamiliarity with shrimp. Tim gives his little smile, "I like those little incongruities." The shrimp scene stayed.

Susan also played a special part in shaping the screenplay. We had long conversations, especially about the conflicts between the nun and the convict. Early on she said, "He needs to be more in your face; he's a manipulator. And you're far too polite with him. You need to get pissed at him when he talks about how he admires Hitler and his other racist crap." She also had a fine-tuned sense of my vulnerability. Especially early on in my relationship with Poncelet she'd point out, "You're too together here. It looks like you have it all figured out. We have to show how unsure you were, how you were in over your head."

One thing about Susan. She's so bloomin' real.

She also lent her touch to the mothers in the story. She was the one who thought of Poncelet's mother showing baby pictures.

She also was the one who knew from the beginning that the story of *Dead Man Walking* is a love story, albeit a different kind of love story. In the end, as Tim edited and pared to the heart of the story, we realized it, too, and in the final editing he pared away whole scenes and subplots and reams of dialogue to unfurl the heart of the story, the encounter and unfolding relationship between two very unlikely people.

It is Tim's genius as a storyteller that let him see through to the heart of this story and to seal it forever in celluloid. I also think it is the key reason why people flock to see the film. It is, of course, a film that makes people feel and think about the death penalty in a way they never have before, but it's the scent of unconditional love that makes people leave the theater feeling uplifted and heartened and saved.

Dead Man Walking

Screenplay by
Tim Robbins

Based on the book Dead Man Walking
by Sister Helen Prejean, C.S.J.

The superscript numbers in the following screenplay correspond to the Scene Notes at the end of the book, which give Tim Robbins's explanation of scene changes and omissions, as well as some fascinating insights into the directorial process.

A Gregorian chant plays hauntingly mixed with the
percussive sounds of a city street.

1   INT. PREJEAN MOTHER'S HOME BEDROOM (1966). DAY.   1

An 8-mm color film from the 60s. Crude homemade credits
say: "Helen's Big Day!" We see a young woman, dressed in a
white bridal gown. She looks up and waves at the camera in
an embarrassed way.

2   EXT. STREETS/INT. PREJEAN CAR. DAY.   2

We are close on the face of SISTER HELEN PREJEAN, a
Catholic nun who belies our standard image of nuns in
movies. She is presently, in fact, anonymous; forgoing the
traditional habit for a practical simple dress. In fact the
only thing suggesting religion is the simple silver
crucifix she wears around her neck. She looks out the
window of the car. Through the car window we pass some
children playing.

3   INT. CATHOLIC CHURCH (1966). DAY.   3

The 8-mm film continues: The young woman in the bridal gown
walks down the aisle of the church, third in a line of six
BRIDES. All the brides are proceeded by little girls who
carry baskets containing black material in front of them.

4   EXT. STREETS/INT. PREJEAN CAR. DAY.   4

We are close on Sister Prejean, her mind elsewhere. We
drift closer to her eyes.

5   INT. CHURCH (1966). DAY.   5

8-mm film: The six brides kneel at the altar as an
Archbishop performs the ceremony.

6   EXT. STREETS/INT. PREJEAN CAR. DAY.   6

Sister Prejean parks the car and runs up a stairwell to an
apartment.

A7   INT. APARTMENT. DAY.   A7

Prejean enters, picks up a shopping bag, and leaves.

7 INT. CHURCH (1966). DAY.   **7**

8-mm film: The brides walk down the aisle toward the front
door, bundles in their hands. The film cuts and the brides
are returning into the church, this time dressed in
traditional black and white habit. We see Helen who, as she
passes the camera, looks directly at us and smiles.

8 EXT. CHURCH (1966). DAY.   **8**

Helen stands with her mother smiling, a nun now. She waves
at the camera. It begins to rain.

9 EXT. STREETS. ST. THOMAS. DAY.   **9**

Prejean walks at a brisk pace carrying a shopping bag. She
has a strong confident walk; this is a woman with work to
do. As she walks we see snatches of the neighborhood. It
has seen better days, but there is a warmth here, a sense
of community.

10 INT. HOPE HOUSE. SUNSET.   **10**

Prejean walks up the front steps, greeting some children
who skip rope. As she enters we see a group of people
waiting for her. One of them, Ruth, addresses her.

                    RUTH
          Well if it ain't the late
          Sister Helen.

                    PREJEAN
          I got a note from my mama.

Laughter.

                    PREJEAN
          I brought y'all some presents.

She takes notebooks and pencils from the shopping bag. A
man comes in and sees Prejean. This is LUIS MONTOYA.

                    MONTOYA
          Sister Helen. Got a second?

                    PREJEAN
          In a minute.

11   INT. PRISON COALITION OFFICE. SUNSET.[1]   11

                    MONTOYA
          Listen, Sister, we've got this
          fella, death-row inmate. He
          could use a pen pal, doesn't
          have anyone. I was wondering if
          you could write to him?

                    PREJEAN
          Sure.

                    MONTOYA
          His name is Matthew Poncelet.

Montoya is writing down the information.

                    MONTOYA
          He's in for murder.

She looks down at the name.

                    MONTOYA
          Maybe I ought to give you
          someone else. This guy is a
          loner and doesn't write. Maybe
          you want someone who will
          answer your letters.

                    PREJEAN
          Nah, don't change it. Give him
          to me.

                    MONTOYA
          He's from Slidell, Louisiana.
          We have files at the office if
          you want to read about the
          case.

She takes the piece of paper with the name on it.

                    PREJEAN
          Look. I gotta go now. Have a
          class. Catch you later, OK?

12   INT. HOPE HOUSE CLASSROOM. NIGHT.   12

Prejean teaches a high school equivalency class. She is
alongside a student who is reading, stumbling over the
words. The rest of the students work quietly at their
desks.

13   INT. PRISON COALITION. NIGHT.   13

Prejean opens a folder labeled "Correspondence." She finds
a letter from Matt, written from jail.

                    MATT (V.O.)
          This lawyer I have, I'm not
          sure what all he's doing for me
          because I hardly ever see him.
          Can you help me?

She turns page. Montoya appears behind her, looking over
her shoulder.

                    MONTOYA
          Of course, none of the guys on
          the row can afford to hire
          their own attorney for their
          appeals; so you can imagine the
          frantic telephone calls we get
          from death-row inmates, begging
          us to find them attorneys.

                    PREJEAN

          Free of charge.

                    MONTOYA
          That's right. These petitions
          take hours and hours to
          prepare. Attorneys aren't
          exactly lining up outside this
          door for the job.

14   INT. PREJEAN APARTMENT. NIGHT.   14

Prejean is finishing writing a letter to Matt Poncelet. We
see her hand as she signs her name and: THREE PHOTOS:

15 Prejean in the woods.   15

16 A color photo of blue, shimmering water at Bay St.   16
Louis, Mississippi.

17 A picture of Christ on the cross.   17

18 INT. PREJEAN APARTMENT (ASH WEDNESDAY). DAY.   18

There is a knock on the door. Prejean's friend and roommate
SISTER COLLEEN opens the door. At the door are three kids.[2]

> KID #1
> Sister, Sister, can we have
> some candy?

> COLLEEN
> How'd you all do on your
> spelling test?

> KID #1
> B plus.

> PREJEAN
> Wow. That's excellent. Colleen,
> we got any candy?

> COLLEEN
> I think I saw some in here
> somewhere.

> PREJEAN
> Hey, we got a new jigsaw
> puzzle. You want to try it?

> KID #1
> Is it one where there's pieces
> missing?

> PREJEAN
> I hope not. Let's try it.

As they do:

> KID #2
> I'm gonna go.

(CONTINUED)

18 CONTINUED: 18

                              COLLEEN

            Take the candy and run, eh?

                              KID #2
            Got homework.

                              KID #3
            You got dirt on your head.

                              PREJEAN
            Those are ashes. It's Ash
            Wednesday.

                              KID #3
            What's that?

                              PREJEAN
            It's a holy day.

                              KID #3
            But why do you put dirt on your
            head?

                              PREJEAN
            Well it's a reminder of our
            mortality.... There's an
            expression; ashes to ashes,
            dust ... it's a way to remember
            God.

                              KID #3
            Oh.

19 INT. PREJEAN APARTMENT. NIGHT.   19

        A gunshot. Prejean wakes up. She gets out of bed, goes to
        the window and sees three teenage boys running from a
        shooting. A body lies on the ground. She quickly goes to
        the phone and dials 911.[3]

                              MATT (V.O.)
                    Dear Sister Helen, Thank you
                    for writing to me. I'm writing
                    from my home, my-six-by-eight-
                    foot cell. I'm in here 23 hours
                    a day, we don't work on death
                    row.

20   EXT. ST. THOMAS PROJECT. NIGHT.   **20**

We see the flashing lights of an ambulance and a police
car. Residents of the project hover and linger. Prejean
consoles a woman as the boy, HERBIE, who was shot is put
into the ambulance, still alive.

> MATT (V.O.)
> We're special here, they keep
> us away from the general
> population of the prison. We're
> the elite, because we're going
> to fry.

21   INT. PREJEAN APARTMENT. DAY.   **21**

INSERT: Photo of Matt Poncelet; a blurred image.

We see Prejean, looking at the photo.

22   EXT. LOUISIANA HIGHWAY. DAY.   **22**

Prejean drives through a light rain. We see a billboard.
It says: "Get tough! Join Governor Fredericks. Stop Crime!"

> MATT (V.O.)
> It's hard not to get soft in
> this cell, I press my
> footlocker, lift it, try to get
> my muscles in shape, but it's
> hard not to get fat. Rice,
> potatoes, pancakes and beans.
> Sometimes I feel like a sow on
> a farm that's being fattened up
> for a Christmas slaughter.

The rain picks up a bit.

23   EXT. ANGOLA PRISON GATE./INT. PREJEAN CAR. DAY.   **23**

She makes a sharp S-curve in the road and sees a clearing,
an open sky, and the Louisiana State Penitentiary - Angola.
Prejean drives up to the front gate. Several armed, blue-
uniformed guards occupy a small, glassed-in office. One of
them comes to the car, and she shows him a letter. They
direct her to Visitor Processing.

24 INT. VISITOR ENTRANCE. DAY.

Prejean walks through a metal detector. It beeps as she
walks through.

> GUARD
> Remove any metal, coins, keys.

Prejean feels her pockets then notices the cross on her
neck. She takes it off and places it in a plastic bin. She
walks through. No beep. A female guard approaches her and
pats her down.

> MATT (V.O.)
> I had a dream once that I was
> about to be fried in the chair
> and a guard came into my cell
> with a chefs hat on and started
> to roll me around in
> breadcrumbs licking his chops
> and all. Maybe you think I'm a
> weirdo to have dreams like that
> but your mind does funny things
> when you're locked up and
> surrounded by people that want
> to kill you. Anyway, thanks for
> writing. I don't get many
> letters. Visitors either. No
> one in my family seems able to
> make the trip out here. I
> understand. It's a long drive
> from Slidell.

25 INT. CHAPLAINS OFFICE. DAY.

Prejean waits. CHAPLAIN FARLEY comes in from one of the
offices along the side wing of the building. His face is
kind, but tired. Farley is a Catholic priest and the chief
chaplain of the prison.

> FARLEY
> Good morning, Sister.

> PREJEAN
> Good morning, Father.

(CONTINUED)

25   CONTINUED: 25

She shakes his hand, firmly. A pause.

> FARLEY
> Have you ever been in a prison
> before?

> PREJEAN
> No. But Sister Clement and I
> sang some songs at a Juvenile
> Detention Center in New
> Orleans.

She laughs.

> PREJEAN
> We sang "Kumbaya," and the boys
> really liked it. They started
> making up their own verses,
> singing, "Someone's escapin' my
> Lord, Kum ..." The guards made
> us sing a different song.

Farley laughs lightly. Then:

> FARLEY
> Where is your habit?

> PREJEAN
> Our sisters haven't worn the
> habit for twenty years.

> FARLEY
> You are aware of the Papal
> request regarding nuns'
> garments aren't you?

> PREJEAN
> The pope said "distinctive
> clothing" not "habits."

> FARLEY
> I'm sure you will interpret it
> your own way. Whatever's
> convenient.

A pause. Farley is looking at a paper on his desk.

                                                            (CONTINUED)

25 CONTINUED: (2)   **25**

>   FARLEY
> Matthew Poncelet. I remember
> him from the news. Him and
> another fella shot two children
> in the back of the head on
> Lover's Lane. Raped the girl
> and stabbed her several times.
> Do you know what you're getting
> into?

Prejean is at a loss for words.

>   FARLEY
> So what is this, Sister? Morbid
> fascination? Bleeding heart
> sympathy?

>   PREJEAN
> No. He wrote me and asked me to
> come.

>   FARLEY
> There is no romance here,
> Sister, no Jimmy Cagney, I've
> been wrongly accused if only I
> had someone who believed in me
> nonsense. This is a bunch of
> con men and they'll take
> advantage of you every way they
> can. You must be very, very
> careful. Do you understand?

>   PREJEAN
> Yes, Father.

>   FARLEY
> These men don't see many
> females. Wearing the habit
> would help instill respect.
> For you to flout authority will
> only encourage them to do the
> same.

26 EXT. ANGOLA PRISON/DEATH-ROW BUILDING. DAY. 26

Prejean waits outside the gate of the fenced-in yard
surrounding the DEATH-ROW BUILDING. A WOMAN GUARD in a
nearby watchtower opens the gate electronically from a
control switch. Sound of a LOUD CLICK. Prejean walks
through and the gate clangs shut behind her.

27 EXT. LOUISIANA WOODS (1988). NIGHT - IMAGINED. 27

We see a car parked. Music plays. Two pairs of legs
approach slowly. Sounds of prison continue.

28 EXT. ANGOLA PRISON. DAY. 28

Prejean walks along, accompanied by a guard. There are
flowers along the sidewalk leading to the building.

29 EXT. LOUISIANA WOODS. NIGHT - IMAGINED. 29

We hear a scream.

      VOICE
    Get out of the car.

30 INT. DEATH-ROW BUILDING. DAY.

Prejean is accompanied by a GUARD through a series of gates
down a hallway.

31 EXT. LOUISIANA WOODS (1988). NIGHT - IMAGINED. 31

A woman is being raped. We see nothing clearly but we feel
the violence and hear the woman weeping.

32 INT. DEATH-ROW BUILDING. DAY. 32

We see Prejean as a guard yells out:

      GUARD
   Woman on the tier!

Gate One: CLANG. Gate Two: CLANG. Gate Three: CLANG. METAL
ON METAL.

33   EXT. LOUISIANA WOODS (1988). NIGHT - IMAGINED.   33

We are TIGHT on a hand with a knife swooping down.

34   INT. DEATH ROW. DAY.   34

It's all green and cement and bars. And it is stiflingly
hot. No circulation in the air. On the front door we see
yellow SCRIPT LETTERS: DEATH ROW.

35   EXT. LOUISIANA WOODS (1988). NIGHT - IMAGINED.   35

We are TIGHT on a gun. It is placed at the base of the
skull. A gunshot.

36   INT. DEATH ROW. DAY.   36

Prejean and a GUARD come to a door, which he unlocks and
opens.

                    GUARD
          Wait here. They'll get your man
          for you.

Prejean steps into room. Guard closes and locks door behind
her. She remains standing in front of door for a moment,
looking around at the room: There are six visiting stalls
the size of telephone booths constructed of plywood painted
white. A heavy mesh screen separates visitors from inmates.
Two other visits are taking place. An older white woman and
a black woman with three kids.

She starts to slowly pace back and forth, trying to take
deep breaths, to settle down.

                  PREJEAN
              (whispers)
          Jesus, help me. What am I
          getting myself into?[4]

She stops when she hears the rattle of chains scraping
across the floor, and A VOICE, laughing and teasing the
guard.

37   EXT. LOUISIANA WOODS (1988). NIGHT - IMAGINED.   37

We see blood. We hear whimpering. Another gun, another
skull. Gunshot.

38   INT. DEATH ROW. DAY.   38

Close on face of Matthew Poncelet.

He is freshly shaven and his brown hair is combed into a
wave in the front. He has a handsome face, open, smiling.
Not the face she had seen in the photo. He has on a blue
denim shirt and jeans. His hands are cuffed to a wide brown
leather belt at his waist.

                    PREJEAN
          Hi Matthew, I made it.

                    MATT (laughing softly)
          Thanks for coming to see me
          ma'am. Never thought I'd be
          visitin' with no nun.

They sit down in one of the booths. There is a pause. He
lights a cigarette. Another pause.

                    MATT
          So, you're a nun.

                    PREJEAN
          Yep.

A pause.

                    PREJEAN
          I want you to know, Matthew,
          that I'm here to listen. We can
          talk about whatever you want.

                    MATT
          You're very sincere.

                    PREJEAN
          What do you mean?

                    MATT
          You've never done this before.

                                        (CONTINUED)

38   CONTINUED:

                    PREJEAN
         No.

                    MATT
         Never been this close to a
         murderer before?

                    PREJEAN
         Not that I know of.

                    MATT
         Well you live in St. Thomas.
         Lots of niggers around there.
         They knock each other off like
         beer cans on a fence.

An awkward pause.

                    MATT
         You know when I first got your
         letter and I seen Helen on it I
         thought it was my first ex-old
         lady. I almost ripped it up.
         She turned me in, told the
         sheriff where to find me.
         Orphaned our kid, the stupid
         bitch.

                    PREJEAN
         You have a kid?

                    MATT
         Yes. A con with a kid.

                    PREJEAN
         Boy or a girl?

                    MATT
         Girl.

                    PREJEAN
         What's her name?

                    MATT
         You have lots of questions.

                                        (CONTINUED)

38   CONTINUED: (2)   38

                         PREJEAN
           I don't know you.

                          MATT
           Well, never mind.

A pause.

                          MATT
           Do I scare you?

A long pause.

                          MATT
           You told me in your letter you
           work with poor people. Your
           daddy was a lawyer? You come
           from money, don't you?

                         PREJEAN
           Some.

                          MATT
           And you live in the St. Thomas
           Projects? I don't get that. I don't
           know who's more crazy. You or me.

                         PREJEAN
           I live where I work.

                          MATT
           In a slum.

                         PREJEAN
           How about you?

                          MATT
           I live here.

                         PREJEAN
           You grew up poor.

                                        (CONTINUED)

38   CONTINUED: (3)

                              MATT
                    Shit. Nobody from money on the Row.

A pause.

                              PREJEAN
                    Then you and I have something in common.

                              MATT
                    What's that?

                              PREJEAN
                    We both live with the poor.

A pause.

                              MATT
                    Ain't you gonna ask me what I did?

                              PREJEAN
                    The Chaplain filled me in.

                              MATT
                    Such a religious man.

Pause.

                              MATT
                    I didn't kill nobody.
                    Carl went crazy on me.

                              PREJEAN
                    Who's Carl?

                              MATT
                    Vitello. He's the one that
                    should be sitting here. He went
                    nuts on me. I was scared. I
                    just did what he said, held
                    the boy back, but he killed
                    them. After it happened we was
                    runnin' around in those woods
                    lost, goin' through brambles
                    and mud and couldn't find the
                    truck.

                                        (CONTINUED)

38   CONTINUED: (4)   38

                              PREJEAN
                    You watched him kill these
                    kids?

                              MATT
                    Truth is me and Carl were
                    loaded on downs, acid, and
                    booze when this happened. I
                    hadn't slept in two nights.
                    It's a blur. I was out of my
                    head. But I didn't kill them. I
                    didn't kill anybody. I swear to
                    God I didn't.

A39   EXT. SUBURBAN STREET (1988). NIGHT - IMAGINED.(OLD 41)   A39

      A Sheriff's Officer is at the door of a house. It is late
      at night. The door opens. A woman opens the door, a blur.

                              TROOPER
                    Ma'am. We found your daughter.

                              MARYBETH (O.S.)
                    Oh my god, no.

B39   INT. DEATH ROW. DAY   B39

      Matt takes out an old tattered photograph. He holds it up
      to the grate. It is a photo of a two-year-old.[5]

                              MATT
                    Allie.

                              PREJEAN
                    Allie?

                              MATT
                    Her name.

                              PREJEAN
                    She's cute.

                                                      (CONTINUED)

                         MATT
          She's eleven ... or twelve. I
          don't know. She was born when I
          was in prison, the first time.
          I seen her once.

                         PREJEAN
          When was that?

                         MATT
          She was three. Got out of
          Marion and went straight to my
          old lady's place in Breaux
          Bridge. I see this beautiful
          girl playing in the front yard,
          grab her up into my arms and
          say, "I'm your daddy!" and I
          look around and there's her
          mother pointing a shotgun at
          me. She's called the cops.
          Thought I was a kidnapper or
          something. She sees it's me,
          puts the gun down, starts
          acting all cold, making rude
          remarks in front of the kid
          about me being a con and all. I
          get real angry, bust up some
          furniture, cops come, chop
          chop, back to jail. That's the
          last I saw of my daughter.

                         PREJEAN
          Do you write to her?

                         MATT
          Don't know where she is. When
          my dumb-ass girlfriend called
          the sheriff on me they didn't
          think too much of her either,
          found some dope in the house,
          took the kid away. She's in
          Texas somewhere. Foster
          parents.

                                        (CONTINUED)

B39 CONTINUED: (2)

A pause.

> GUARD
> Wrap it up, Sister.

We start on Prejean.

> MATT
> They about to go on a killin'
> spree. Zappin' this dude Tobias
> tonight. The guards been taking
> bets on who's next. I'm at even
> odds. Not good. The way I see
> it I got two chances. The
> pardon board and a federal
> appeals court. I can write the
> motion and all, I just need
> someone to file it.

> PREJEAN
> You a lawyer?

> MATT
> When your back is against the
> wall you learn the law fast.
> Let's just say you have special
> motivation. I've been on death
> row for six years, been reading
> and studying every law book I
> can get my hands on.

A clang is heard, the door opening, a guard appears. Matt
holds a folder.

> MATT
> Look, I got a whole lot of
> stuff about my case,
> transcripts of my trials and
> legal papers. Maybe they would
> help you get a hold of things
> about me and my case faster.

(CONTINUED)

B39   CONTINUED: (3)   **B39**

An awkward pause.

> MATT
> You ain't coming back are you?

> PREJEAN
> No, I was just ... are these
> your only copies?

> MATT
> I got my own copy. But they
> hard to come by so if you ain't
> gonna help me I don't want to
> waste 'em on you.

> PREJEAN
> I'll look them over. I
> appreciate your trust.

> MATT
> I tell you what, ma'am, I sure
> as hell don't trust nobody
> around this place. You didn't
> come here to kiss my ass and
> preach all that hellfire and
> brimstone crap. I respect that.
> You're alright. You got guts.
> You live in a neighborhood
> where every nigger has a gun.
> Appreciate your visit though,
> ma'am. Thanks for listening,
> and for making the long trip.

> PREJEAN
> No trouble.

> MATT
> And you be careful on your
> drive home. People are crazy
> out there.

(CONTINUED)

B39 CONTINUED: (4)   B39

Matt continues to talk but the words are unintelligible.
Through the screen his image is distorted, then a blur.

Poncelet is led away. Clang. Prejean lets out a sigh of
relief.

39   EXT. LOUISIANA WOODS (1988). NIGHT - IMAGINED.   39

We drift slowly along the tall brush, the sound of cicadas
hypnotizingly loud. We see a torn garment, a shoe, and then
a hand which leads us to two dead bodies lying grotesquely
askew.

40   OMITTED   40

41   OMITTED   41

42   OMITTED   42

43   EXT. LOUISIANA HIGHWAY/INT. PREJEAN CAR. DAY.   43

Prejean drives, deep in thought.

44   OMITTED   44

45   OMITTED   45

A46 EXT. LOUISIANA WOODS (1988). NIGHT - IMAGINED.   A46

A LONG LENS SHOT of Poncelet and Vitello running through
the woods.

46   EXT. PREJEAN MOTHER'S HOME (1955). DAY - FLASHBACK.   46

Six boys and a young girl are chasing a possum. The kids
surround the animal. It lays down and "plays possum." One
of the boys approaches the animal with a stick and hits it.
We see the little girl and hear the stick hitting the
possum again and again.[6]

                         KID #1 (V.O.)
               Is he dead?

                         KID #2
               Playin' possum, huh? You think
               you can trick us you dumb
               animal.

                                              (CONTINUED)

46   CONTINUED: 46

He hits the animal.

                        KID #2
              Think you can fool us?

Another kid hits the animal. Then another.

                        KID #1
              It's your turn Helen.

Eight-year-old Helen Prejean picks up the stick and
approaches the animal, draws up the stick and brings it
down on the bleeding animal. We see the face of the eight-
year-old.

A47 EXT. LOUISIANA WOODS (1988). DAY - IMAGINED.   A47

We see the body of two kids surrounded by policemen.
Flashbulbs, a low, sober murmur. We hear a siren and see a
flashing red light.

47   EXT. LOUISIANA HIGHWAY./INT. PREJEAN CAR. DAY.   47

Prejean is being pulled over by a state trooper.

                        TROOPER
              License and registration.

Prejean complies.

                        PREJEAN
              How fast was I going?

                        TROOPER
              85 MPH.

                        PREJEAN
              Wow.

                        TROOPER
              You a nun?

                        PREJEAN
              Yes.

                                        (CONTINUED)

47 CONTINUED: **47**

> TROOPER
> Ain't never gave a ticket to no
> nun before. You ain't gonna say
> no bad prayers about me are
> you?

> PREJEAN
> No sir.

> TROOPER
> Gave a ticket to a guy from the
> IRS, got audited the next year.
> Tell you what, I think I'm
> gonna pass on this one. Just
> keep your speed down, OK?

48 INT. PRISON COALITION. DAY.[7]   **48**

Prejean with Luis Montoya.

> PREJEAN
> Poncelet claims that Vitello
> killed them both. Y'all think
> he's lying?

> MONTOYA
> Vitello accuses Poncelet. Both
> say the other did the actual
> killing. Somebody's lying to
> somebody.

> PREJEAN
> Well how is it possible that
> one man gets life and one gets
> death?

> MONTOYA
> The State only goes after death
> in one out of fifty cases.

> PREJEAN
> Why's that?

> MONTOYA
> Too expensive. Costs two
> million to kill a man, half a
> mil to keep him in for life.
> (MORE)

(CONTINUED)

CONTINUED:

                    MONTOYA (CONT'D)
          State probably had a stronger
          case against Poncelet or
          Vitello had a better lawyer,
          was able to create doubt in the
          jury's mind.

                    PREJEAN
          And Vitello gets life, Poncelet
          death.

                    MONTOYA
          Yep.

                    PREJEAN
          Bad luck.

                    MONTOYA
          He needs help, Helen. There is
          a lawyer by the name of Hilton
          Barber. He's aware of the case,
          told me no. Maybe you could
          change his mind.

                    PREJEAN
          With the aim of getting him a
          new trial? What if he gets off?
          I'm not sure I'd want to run
          into this guy on the street.

                    MONTOYA
          There's no way he's going to
          get off. He was there. He was
          an accomplice, and that's life.
          Life sentences in Louisiana are
          for real. We're just trying to
          keep the State from killing
          him. Listen, you want out,
          that's cool with me. You don't
          have to go back there.

                    PREJEAN
          I'd like to read more about it.

                    MONTOYA
          I've got a file. I'll give you
          that.

                                        (CONTINUED)

48 CONTINUED: (2)   **48**

> PREJEAN
> Luis, do you know if Hope Percy
> was an only child?

> MONTOYA
> What?

> PREJEAN
> I'm just thinking of her mama
> and daddy. God! How do they put
> their heads on their pillows at
> night knowing what happened to
> their daughter?

49 INT. PREJEAN APARTMENT. NIGHT.[8]   **49**

Sister Colleen is cooking in the kitchen.

> COLLEEN
> You've been to another country,
> huh girl?

> PREJEAN
> Another planet, Colleen. What
> you got there, mustard greens?

> COLLEEN
> Uh huh.

> PREJEAN
> How's Herbie doing?

> COLLEEN
> He's OK. You know his shooting
> wasn't in the paper.

> PREJEAN
> It wasn't?

> COLLEEN
> We called them. Called all the
> TV stations, too. Figure they'd
> want to know when a twelve-
> year-old kid gets shot.
> Not a word. I guess we don't
> exist here in St. Thomas.

50 INT. PREJEAN APARTMENT. MORNING.[9]   **50**

We start on the radio, then see Sister Colleen and Helen having coffee.

> RADIO
> The execution, which was
> originally scheduled for
> midnight was dramatically
> halted as Tobias approached the
> chair. Tobias returned to his
> cell where he waited for an
> hour while a legal question was
> being discussed. At 1:00 A.M.
> the convicted murderer was
> removed from his cell and
> brought once again to the
> electric chair, where he was
> executed.

We see a radio in TIGHT SHOT.

> RADIO
> Tobias was pronounced dead at
> 1:15 A.M. Tobias will be the
> last to die in Gruesome Gertie,
> the state's electric chair. An
> execution scheduled in five
> weeks will usher in the use of
> lethal injection in the State
> of Louisiana. This is Accu-
> News.

Instantly a shock jock comes on. This is PURVIS SLADE. We pull away from the radio to see Colleen and Prejean standing by it, listening. "Happy Days Are Here Again" plays as:

> SLADE (V.O.)
> Zap! Goodnight Mr. Tobias.
> Guess you shouldn't have messed
> around in the State of
> Louisiana.

He plays a sound effect of electricity. Colleen switches the station. Another news report on the execution. Prejean looks down at the floor. Sitting there is the file that Matt gave her and the file of clippings from Montoya. She picks up the clippings.

51 INT. PREJEAN APARTMENT. DAY.   **51**

We are CLOSE on the headlines of the murder. We see Prejean and
Sister Colleen looking through the file. We see pictures of
CLYDE PERCY, MARYBETH PERCY, and EARL DELACROIX. Their faces
hold an immense grief. These are the parents of the victims. We
see inserts of various newspaper clippings, photographs, and
letters. Also, overlapping voices read from newspaper articles.

52 INSERT: FRONT PAGE HEADLINE OF THE SLIDELL   **52**
JOURNAL; JUNE 20, 1988: "LEADS ARE FEW IN TEENAGE MURDER
HERE." PHOTO; SMILING FACES OF A TEENAGE COUPLE.[10]

                    REPORTER #1
          On Friday night, Walter
          Delacroix, aged 17, and Hope
          Percy, 18, had been just two
          happy people celebrating one of
          life's turning points....

                    REPORTER #2
          The couple had been shot twice
          at close range in the back of
          the head with a .22-caliber
          rifle.

53 INSERT: FRONT PAGE HEADLINE OF THE JOURNAL; JULY 12,   **53**
1988: PHOTO FEATURES: SNEERING FACES OF THE MURDERERS
MATTHEW PONCELET, 26, AND CARL VITELLO, 31.

                    REPORTER #3
          In addition to murder charges,
          Poncelet and Vitello face six
          counts of aggravated kidnapping
          and one charge of aggravated
          rape. In the four weeks before
          the murders, the two accused
          men allegedly had cut a wide
          path of terror across the area,
          attacking several teenage
          couples in local lovers' lanes.

54   INSERT: VIDEO: Poncelet when first arrested,   54
      with wild, long tangled hair.

                         REPORTER #4
                    Poncelet and Vitello, posing as
                    security guards, would handcuff
                    the men and molest the women.
                    Most of the couples were too
                    ashamed to come forward. A
                    police spokesman said today
                    that in the wake of the
                    killings several couples have
                    courageously revealed what
                    happened to them and have
                    identified Poncelet and Vitello
                    as the assailants.

                         VOICE
                    ...drew his hand menacingly
                    like a knife across his throat
                    when Joseph Dunham appeared in
                    the courtroom....

                         VOICE
                    When Dunham's girlfriend
                    appeared, a young woman
                    Poncelet had raped, he winked
                    and blew her a kiss...

55   INSERT: PHOTOGRAPH and VIDEO: Poncelet, hands and feet   55
      cuffed, looking at Vitello and grinning as they walk into
      the courthouse.

                         VOICE
                    Matthew Poncelet addressed the
                    judge as "Cap" and smirked when
                    the jury found him guilty of
                    murder today....

                         VOICE
                    ...told his weeping mother to
                    "dry up."

56   INSERT: PHOTOGRAPH AND VIDEO: Poncelet with a bandanna on   56
      his head, caught close up by the camera, sneering.

57   OMITTED   57

58   INT. PREJEAN APARTMENT. NIGHT.   **58**

TITLE: THREE WEEKS LATER

Prejean watches the television news. Poncelet's face is on
it. The phone rings.[II]

                    PREJEAN
          Hello.

                    MATT (V.O.)
          Sister Helen?

                    PREJEAN
          Who's this?

                    MATT (V.O.)
          Matt Poncelet. Sister, I didn't
          know who to call. I know I'm on
          death row but there's guys been
          here for years. I didn't know
          this was coming. They set a
          date.

                    PREJEAN
          I just saw.

                    MATT (V.O.)
          They're gonna kill me. I gotta
          do something. I didn't know
          you need a lawyer to get a
          pardon board hearing, hell I'd
          do it myself if they'd let me,
          but they say, "No lawyer, no
          hearing."

A pause. Helen is speechless.

                    PREJEAN
          OK, OK, Matthew, keep your
          cool. I'll think of something.
          I've heard of a lawyer who can
          maybe help you, Matthew. I'll
          see what I can do.

                                        (CONTINUED)

58 CONTINUED: **58**

> MATT (V.O.)
> Sister, come through for me.
> You all I got. They got me on a
> greased rail to the death
> house. I ain't heard from you.
> You ain't fadin' out on me are
> you, Sis?

> PREJEAN
> I'll get you that lawyer,
> Matthew. Try not to worry.

She hangs up the phone and we hear distant gunshots.

59 INSERT: TV SET.   **59**

On the television we see the gurney and the lethal
injection machine. We see Fredericks and then, surprise, a
photo of Matt Poncelet. Clyde Percy, the father of Hope
Percy is being interviewed.

> CLYDE (ON TV)
> It's been six years and it's
> about time they got on with it.
> I would have preferred seeing
> him fry. Call me sentimental.

60 INT. PREJEAN APARTMENT. NIGHT.   **60**

Prejean is looking for a phone number, she finds it and
dials the number.

> PREJEAN
> Luis, What was the name of that
> lawyer you wanted me to talk
> to?

61 EXT. LOUISIANA HIGHWAY/INT. PREJEAN CAR. DAY.   **61**

Prejean drives with HILTON BARBER.[12]

> HILTON
> We got a chance here with Poncelet. I
> found a ton of legal procedural
> errors in his trial transcript. His
> (MORE)

(CONTINUED)

61 CONTINUED: **61**

> HILTON (CONT'D)
> lawyer was bush league, an amateur,
> met Poncelet a day before his trial.
> Jury selection took four hours. Trial
> lasted five days. His lawyer raised
> one objection in the entire trial.

We see a crude handmade sign off the road "Have Many Rabbit."

> HILTON
> Have many rabbit.

> PREJEAN
> Is that a for sale sign or a
> plea for help?

He laughs.

> HILTON
> Or is he braggin'?

> PREJEAN
> Imagine that poor guy. Buys two
> rabbits a year ago and now he's
> overrun.

He laughs.

> HILTON
> Got 'em comin' like popcorn.

A pause.

> HILTON
> How long have you been doing
> this Sister?

> PREJEAN
> This?

> HILTON
> Counseling death-row inmates.

(CONTINUED)

61 CONTINUED: (2)

> PREJEAN
> I'm not counseling him. I
> barely know him, only met him
> once.

> HILTON
> Well, what's your impression,
> Sister?

> PREJEAN
> I don't know if I like him. But
> he needs help. Best way I can
> figure is to bring you to him.

> HILTON
> Well, I'll do my best. You like
> sports?

> PREJEAN
> I like baseball.

> HILTON
> You know what it's like to
> follow a team that has a hard
> time winning.

> PREJEAN
> Oh yeah. I'm a Mudhen fan.

> HILTON
> Mudhen?

> PREJEAN
> My high school team. We had a
> perfect record my senior year.
> 0-19.

> HILTON
> Well, we do a little better
> than that. But that's the idea.
> That's what it's like, this
> business. You see, the courts
> don't want to hear appeals on
> death penalty cases. Hell, you
> can even have new evidence of
> (MORE)

(CONTINUED)

61 CONTINUED: (3)   61

                              HILTON (CONT'D)
                    innocence and the courts won't
                    hear the case. We're the
                    pariahs. We're holding up the
                    court system. We're bleeding
                    hearts. There it is.

He is pointing to the sign nailed high up in the tree.
Helen reads:

                              PREJEAN
                    Do not despair, you will soon be there.

                              HILTON
                    Somebody knows this road real,
                    real well.

62 INT. DEATH ROW. DAY.   62

Hilton stops at the guard station. He pulls out a twenty
dollar bill.

                              HILTON
                    This is for Poncelet's inmate
                    account. Let me have a receipt.

As they wait for the receipt:

                              HILTON
                    They need cigarettes and
                    coffee. I think smoking is bad,
                    but if you're going to die
                    prematurely why not take the
                    edge off?

                              GUARD
                    Sister Prejean? Hilton Barber?

                              HILTON
                    Yessir.

                                              (CONTINUED)

62 CONTINUED: **62**

> GUARD
> This way.

63 INT. DEATH ROW. DAY. **63**

> MATT
> And the day before Governor
> Benedict says he's runnin' for
> reelection, surprise! A big
> announcement with lots of press
> setting a date for my execution
> to show how tough he is on
> crime.

> HILTON
> Well, I agree with you, Matt.
> Politics did play a big part in
> this decision, but the pardon
> board is not the place to bring
> this up.

> MATT
> Why not?

> HILTON
> Because it's full of political
> appointees, the governor's
> appointees, and the last thing
> they want to hear is some
> convicted killer telling them
> they is bunk. What we have to
> do, Matt, is to present you as
> a human being and convince them
> to spare your life.

> MATT
> What we have to do is prove I
> am innocent.

(CONTINUED)

CONTINUED:

                        HILTON
            We'll get to that. We're filing
            appeals in federal court and
            the Supreme Court. But this is
            the pardon board; don't mean a
            thing to them if you pulled the
            trigger or not. They're
            thinking of the crime and you
            as a monster. It's easy to kill
            a monster but it's hard to kill
            a human being. We need people
            that know you to speak on your
            behalf. Your mama should be at
            this hearing.

                        MATT
            I don't want her there. She's
            just going to bust out cryin'
            and won't be able to say
            nothin' 'cause she's gonna be
            so tore up.

                        HILTON
            Be that as it may, your mama
            should still be there.

                        MATT
            No. No. She's gonna have to sit
            there and hear the Delacroixs,
            the Percys and the D.A.

                        PREJEAN
            Excuse me for butting in. She's
            your mama, Matt, your mama.
            It's going to be upsetting for
            her, but I think she should
            have the opportunity to speak
            for her child if she wants to.

                        MATT
            She's just gonna blubber her
            head off.

                                    (CONTINUED)

63 CONTINUED: (2)   **63**

                    PREJEAN
          Yeah, but she has the right to
          do that. What if you die and
          she didn't have the chance to
          speak for you? Don't you think
          that's going to eat at her?
          She's always going to wonder
          if she could have saved you.

                    MATT
          Yeah...I'll think about it. I
          want y'all to know I got my
          pride. I ain't kissin' ass in
          front of those people. I ain't
          kissin' nobody's ass.

64 EXT. ANGOLA PRISON GATE/PARKING LOT. DAY.[13]   **64**

Prejean and Barber exit the prison.

                    HILTON
          I'm trying to arrange a meeting
          with the head of the pardon
          board. I'm also working on
          cornering the governor. If I
          get a meeting with him I'll
          want you there with me.

                    PREJEAN
          Me? I think you're barking up
          the wrong tree.

                    HILTON
          I can't do this on my own,
          Sister. I need your help.

                    PREJEAN
          I'm not qualified to talk to
          the governor.

                                        (CONTINUED)

64 CONTINUED: 64

                              HILTON
                    OK. You get his mama for me.
                    You qualified to talk to mamas?

                              PREJEAN
                    I'll help you get his mama to
                    the hearing if Matt agrees to
                    it.

                              HILTON
                    We don't have time to wait on
                    this. Trust me. I've been
                    through this pardon board a few
                    times. There's an unwritten
                    rule: No mama, no hearing.

                              PREJEAN
                    I'll go to see his mama now,
                    but it's still up to him
                    whether she goes.

                              HILTON
                    Good deal, Sister. Good deal.

65 INT. PREJEAN APARTMENT. DUSK.   65

It is raining. Three Kids and Colleen are playing in the
living room. Prejean is cutting the pictures of the Percys
and the Delacroixs from a newspaper clipping. She puts them
near her prayer corner on her trunk near a candle, an icon
of Mary, a crucifix, and a Bible.

66 OMITTED   66

67 OMITTED   67

A68 INT. CHURCH (EASTER SUNDAY). DAY.   A68

African American Church.[14] Sunday Mass. Gospel choir.
Colleen is there. We see a crucifix, and ZOOM in on Jesus'
face, a face filled with pain and anguish but somehow kind
and forgiving. Over the choir we see:

68   EXT. DILAPIDATED HOUSE. (EASTER SUNDAY). DAY.   68

Prejean approaches the house. The walkway is overgrown, old tires and abandoned wagons lay strewn about. Prejean knocks on the door. No answer. Then:

> VOICE (V.O.)
> Yes?

> PREJEAN
> Mrs. Poncelet?

> VOICE (V.O.)
> No.

> PREJEAN
> Mrs. Poncelet?

> VOICE (V.O.)
> Don't live here. Who is it?

> PREJEAN
> My name is Sister Helen
> Prejean. I know your son.

A pause.

> LUCILLE (V.O.)
> My son don't know any Sisters.
> What do you want?

> PREJEAN
> Just to talk. Can you open the
> door?

> LUCILLE (V.O.)
> You really a Sister?

> PREJEAN
> Yes.

> LUCILLE (V.O.)
> You're not from the TV?

> PREJEAN
> No.

(CONTINUED)

68 CONTINUED: 68

> LUCILLE(V.O.)
> You sure?

> PREJEAN
> Yes.

The door opens slowly, cautiously. As we see LUCILLE she
flinches as if expecting to be hit. She looks at Prejean
suspiciously.

> LUCILLE
> How do you know Mattie?

> PREJEAN
> I met your son on death row.

> LUCILLE
> Come in.

69 INT. PONCELET HOUSE (EASTER SUNDAY). DAY.[15]   69

> LUCILLE
> You never know who is at your
> front door. I get a lot of
> attention, you know? Everybody
> knows who I am. So what do you
> want? Mattie send you to get
> money for cigarettes?

> PREJEAN
> No.

> LUCILLE
> Well, that's a first. Why you
> here?

> PREJEAN
> You know that they have set a
> date for Matt's execution?

> LUCILLE
> Yeh. Got a call from the
> prison. Said if it goes down do
> I got death insurance? What a
> laugh. I ain't even got food
> money.

(CONTINUED)

69   CONTINUED: 69

                              PREJEAN
                    Matt goes before the pardon
                    board this week. His lawyer
                    thinks it would be a good idea
                    for you to be there.

                              LUCILLE
                    What does Mattie think?

                              PREJEAN
                    He's worried. He wants to
                    protect you.

                              LUCILLE
                    Well, it's a little late for that.

There is a pause. In the living room we see three boys on
the couch watching television.

                              LUCILLE
                    That show, Inside Crime made a
                    show about Mattie and they told
                    how I tried to help him and
                    all, a regular Ma Barker or
                    something. Now I'm famous. I
                    was in a store yesterday and I
                    seen these two ladies eyeing me
                    and I get closer to them I hear
                    one of them say, "I just can't
                    wait to hear that they have
                    executed that monster, Mattie
                    Poncelet." "That's the mother
                    of that killer!" they say.

                              PREJEAN
                    That's cruel.

                              LUCILLE
                    But they're right. I don't
                    know. They think I wasn't there
                    for him. They think I taught
                    him to kill.

A pause.

                                                     (CONTINUED)

69   CONTINUED: (2)   69

                              LUCILLE
                    What do you think, Sister? You
                    think I look like the mother of
                    a killer?

She lights a cigarette. Hands Helen a picture.

                              LUCILLE
                    That's Mattie when he was six.

A pause.

                              LUCILLE
                    Sometimes I want to pretend I'm
                    not his mother so people will
                    leave me alone, not hate me.
                    That's terrible, huh?

                              PREJEAN
                    It's a lot you're asking of
                    yourself. You remember the
                    story of Peter and the cocks
                    crowing?

                              LUCILLE
                    He denied Jesus.

                              PREJEAN
                    That was a good friend of
                    Jesus. Someone he trusted.

                              LUCILLE
                    The rock of the Church.

                              PREJEAN
                    He was scared. It's hard when
                    everyone is screaming for blood.

                              LUCILLE
                    My boys are having a hard time
                    in school. Kids is pickin' on
                    them, beatin' them up, callin'
                    them names. Someone put a dead
                    squirrel in my little Troy's
                    locker. He came home cryin',
                    poor boy. What did he ever do
                    to anybody?

                                              (CONTINUED)

69 CONTINUED: (3)   **69**

A pause.

> LUCILLE
> I keep tryin' to figure out
> what I done wrong.

A70 EXT. PREJEAN HOUSE (EASTER SUNDAY). DUSK.   **A70**

A well-appointed middle class Southern home.

70 INT. PREJEAN HOME (EASTER SUNDAY). DUSK.   **70**

Heirloom dinnerware and tablecloths, everyone seated at the
table, well dressed. Prejean eats dinner with her MOTHER,
her SISTER and her HUSBAND and BABY, and her BROTHER and
his WIFE and their three KIDS.

> PREJEAN
> These people've been plowed
> over by life. Matt gets in
> trouble with the law when he's
> fifteen.

> BROTHER
> Every kid gets in trouble when
> he's fifteen.

> PREJEAN
> His daddy was never around.

> BROTHER
> Helen, most of your kids in the
> projects are raised by single
> parents, and they're not raping
> and killing people. Really
> Helen, you're getting suckered.

> SISTER
> Hush up, Louie.

> BROTHER
> What about the parents of the
> victims? Have you seen them?
> Are you counseling them?

(CONTINUED)

70 CONTINUED: 70

                              PREJEAN
                    Do you think they'd want to see
                    me?

Prejean's mother, who has been listening to all this,
interrupts.

                              MOTHER
                    Helen, why are you doing this?

There is an awkward stillness at the table.

                              MOTHER
                    Aren't there people in your
                    neighborhood that need your
                    help? Honest people?

                              PREJEAN
                    I'm still working with them.

                              MOTHER
                    But why are you visiting with
                    murderers? They're the end of
                    the line people. For all the
                    energy and resources you're
                    putting into them you could be
                    keeping other kids from going
                    to prison and death row.

A pause.

                              SISTER
                    Mom's friends the Pierres read
                    an article where they mentioned
                    your name as being associated
                    with Poncelet.

                              PREJEAN
                    My name was in the paper?

                              MOTHER
                    It has nothing to do with that.
                    I am simply curious, Helen.
                    What has drawn you to this?

                                                    (CONTINUED)

70   CONTINUED: (2)   70

                         PREJEAN
          I don't know, Mama. I feel
          caught more than drawn.[16] This
          man needs help and for some
          reason I'm the only one he
          trusts.

                         MOTHER
          I know your heart's in the
          right place, Helen, but a full
          heart shouldn't follow an empty
          head.

                         BROTHER
          Or an empty stomach.

                         MOTHER
          When you were a child you were
          always bringing home strays. If
          we had taken in all those dogs
          and cats we wouldn't have had
          any money to feed the children
          in this house. Your heart is
          large. Just take care that
          others don't take advantage of
          it. I would hate to see that.

71   EXT. PERCY HOUSE. DAY.[17]   71

Prejean pulls up to the house and gets out of the car. She
starts up the walk and then through the window sees:

72   INT. PERCY HOUSE. DAY.   72

Marybeth Percy, sitting on the couch, staring at the wall.

73   EXT. PERCY HOUSE. DAY.   73

Prejean stops. And turns back.

74   INT. DEATH ROW. DAY.   74

Two families are visiting. Three kids play. Matt is on a
roll. Prejean listens.

                                              (CONTINUED)

74 CONTINUED: **74**

>   MATT
> My Daddy took me to a bar when
> I was twelve and told me pick
> your whiskey, and there was all
> these bottles behind the bar
> and I pointed and said I'd take
> the one with the pretty turkey
> on it. Them guys in the bar
> laughed they butts off.

He Laughs.

>   MATT
> We got drunk as a couple of
> coots that night, boy. Daddy
> was a good man, a sharecropper,
> worked hard. That's one thing I
> got from him. Working hands.

>   PREJEAN
> How old were you when he died?

>   MATT
> Fourteen.

There is a pause.

>   MATT
> Why's you a nun?

A pause.

>   PREJEAN
> I was drawn to it, I guess.
> That's a hard question. Like
> asking you why you're a
> convict.

>   MATT
> Bad luck.

>   PREJEAN
> Then good luck. I had a loving
> family, a lot of support. I
> guess I felt obliged to give
> some of it back.

(CONTINUED)

74 CONTINUED: (2)   **74**

> MATT
> Don't you miss having a man?
> Don't you want to fall in love,
> get married? Have sex?

A Pause.

> MATT
> What? You don't want to talk
> about it?

> PREJEAN
> I have close friends--men and
> women. I haven't experienced
> sexual intimacy with anyone.
> But there are other ways to be
> close. Sharing your feelings
> and thoughts . . . your dreams;
> that's, intimacy, too.

> MATT
> We got intimacy right now, you
> and me. Don't we, Sister?

He snickers. She gives him a hard look.

> PREJEAN
> I went to see your mother.
> She's willing to go to the
> pardon board tomorrow if you'll
> have her.

> MATT
> I like being alone with you.
> You're looking real good to me.

> PREJEAN
> Look at you. Death is breathing
> down your neck and here you
> are, playing you lil' Matt-on-
> the-make-games. I'm not here
> for your amusement, Matt so
> have some respect.

> MATT
> Why should I respect you?
> Because you a nun and wear a
> cross around your neck?

(CONTINUED)

74 CONTINUED: (3)

> PREJEAN
> Because I'm a person, Matt, and
> we all deserve respect. Now
> what's your answer? What's it
> going to be with your mama?

75 INT. PARDON BOARD HEARING ROOM. DAY.[18]

Lucille Poncelet sits by her son without looking at him. He
doesn't look at her either; nor does she touch him. They
both look at a spot on the table in front of them. She
holds an envelope. We see TV cameras, monitors, flashes.

> LUCILLE
> Mattie's had a hard life....

She stops and her eyes fill with tears and she puts her
head down into her arms and tries to continue...

> LUCILLE
> But he was a good boy....

And bursts into uncontrolled sobbing. HENRY, Hilton's
assistant, gets up, takes her by the arm, and leads her out
of the room. Prejean follows them. Hilton rises.

> HILTON
> Ladies and gentlemen, imagine
> this scenario: Man takes
> another man, puts him in a
> locked room, says to him:
> You're gonna die. I ain't gonna
> tell you when, could be
> tomorrow, could be in a week,
> but you're gonna die. Man stays
> in that room, terrified, his
> life on a wire.

76 INT. HALLWAY OUTSIDE PARDON ROOM. DAY.

Prejean holds Lucille in her arms and lets her sob.

> LUCILLE
> I'm sorry. I'm sorry. I'm sorry...

(CONTINUED)

76   CONTINUED: **76**

                        PREJEAN
              Nothing to be sorry about. You
              just let it go.

As she does, we HOLD on the two women as we hear:

                        HILTON (V.O.)
              Six years pass. Man comes into
              the room, says, you're gonna
              die in a week. Plead your case.
              In any court in the land this
              would be considered torture,
              cruel and unusual mental
              torture. This man that kept the
              other in the room would be
              considered a psycho, a madman.
              This man is the State, ladies
              and gentlemen.

                        LUCILLE
              Go back in there, Sister.
              Mattie needs somebody there.

                        HILTON (V.O.)
              The death penalty. It's nothing
              new. Been around for centuries.

Helen gets up to go.

77   INT. PARDON BOARD HEARING ROOM. DAY.   **77**

We see Matt listening. Helen enters and sits next to him.

                        HILTON
              Used to nail people's hands and
              feet to wood, then lash their
              sides and bleed them.
              Throughout the centuries we
              buried people alive, lopped
              their heads off with an axe, a
              guillotine, burned them in
              public squares, gruesome
              spectacle all.
                        (MORE)

                                              (CONTINUED)

CONTINUED:

> HILTON (CONT'D)
> In this century in the search
> for more humane ways to execute
> we have hung people from the
> gallows, shot them in firing
> squads, suffocated them in the
> gas chamber and cooked them
> alive in the electric chair.
> We've got something even more
> "humane" now. Lethal injection.
> We strap the guy up,
> anesthetize him with shot
> number one, then give him shot
> number two that implodes the
> lungs, then shot number three
> that stops the heart. We put
> him to death like an old horse.
> His face just goes to sleep
> while inside his organs are
> going through Armageddon.

A78   INT. HALLWAY OUTSIDE PARDON ROOM. DAY.   A78

We see Lucille, alone.

> HILTON (V.O.)
> His muscles would seize up and
> twitch and contort and pull,
> but shot number one relaxes all
> those muscles. So we don't have
> to see any horror show. We
> don't have to taste the blood
> of ruthlessness on our lips.
> While this human being's organs
> writhe and twist.

B78   INT. PARDON BOARD ROOM. DAY.   B78

Prejean is looking at photos from Lucille's envelope;
photos of Matt as a boy.

> HILTON
> We just sit there and nod our
> heads and say, "Justice has
> been done." The State of
> Louisiana does not have to kill
> Matthew Poncelet to protect its
> citizens.

> (MORE)

(CONTINUED)

B78   CONTINUED: **B78**

> HILTON (CONT'D)
> This man is locked away for the
> rest of his days at Angola
> Prison. He's not getting out.
> We can protect society without
> imitating the very violence we
> seek to eliminate. Let us have
> dignity. Please, let us not be
> complicit in the butchery of
> another human life.

Some board members are fidgety, rustling papers.

> MIRABEAU
> Mr. Gilardi, is the State ready
> to present its case?

Guy Gilardi, the assistant D.A. approaches.

> GILARDI
> Ladies and gentlemen, why does the
> State call for the death penalty in
> the case of Matthew Poncelet? Well,
> let's take a look.

He passes out pictures of the slain teenagers for the board
members to see. We see them; horrible, graphic, bloody.

> GILARDI
> It has been six years since the
> brutal and reprehensible
> murders of Hope Percy and
> Walter Delacroix, and justice
> is long past due. Matt
> Poncelet has had a lengthy,
> thorough court review, not only
> a trial but a retrial for
> sentencing, as well as numerous
> appeals to state and federal
> courts and successor petitions
> filed by Mr. Barber, quite
> obviously a most excellent
> attorney at the service of Mr.
> Poncelet. There has been no
> doubt in the court's mind at
> any time about who did the
> murder. Matthew Poncelet was
> not a good boy.

> (MORE)

(CONTINUED)

B78   CONTINUED: (2)   **B78**

                              GILARDI (CONT'D)
            He was a heartless killer.
            These murders were calculated,
            disgusting, and cruel. This man
            shot Walter Delacroix two times
            in the back of his head, then
            raped Hope Percy and stabbed
            her seventeen times before
            shooting this sweet girl two
            times in the back of the head.
            Since the murder Matthew
            Poncelet has shown no remorse.
            In the courtroom when he was
            sentenced he was smiling and
            chewing his gum. He is an
            unfeeling, perverse misfit and
            it is time, way past time, for
            Mr. Poncelet to pay the
            consequences of his horrifying
            deed.

Gilardi points at the Percys and Delacroix.

                              GILARDI
            These families will never see
            their children graduate from
            college, they will never attend
            their wedding, they will never
            have a Christmas with them
            again. There will be no
            grandchildren. All they ask of
            you is simple justice for their
            unbearable loss.

We see the still, dead face of Walter Delacroix. We see
Delacroix, the Percys.

                              GILARDI
            You have a responsibility to these
            families and you have a
            responsibility to society at large
            to show that horrible crimes have
            horrible consequences. It is only
            through deterrence that we can
            prevent this happening again. I ask
            you to take a breath, steel your
            spine, and proceed with the
            execution of Matthew Poncelet.

78   EXT. PARDON BOARD BUILDING. DAY.   **78**

In the bright white sunshine, clutches of people stand
about on sidewalk. Prejean stands with Hilton.

> HILTON
> You know I don't think anyone
> on this board thinks he's
> innocent. Our only hope is that
> they realize their own
> culpability in the death of a
> man.

> PREJEAN
> You did well in there.

> HILTON
> It's always a good sign when
> you have to wait. Excuse me,
> Sister.

Earl Delacroix approaches.

> DELACROIX
> I'm Walter Delacroix's father.

> PREJEAN
> Oh, Mr. Delacroix, I'm so sorry
> about your son.

> DELACROIX
> Sister, I'm a Catholic. How can
> you sit by Matt Poncelet's side
> without ever having come to
> visit with me and my wife or
> the Percys to hear our side?
> How can you spend all your time
> worrying about Poncelet and not
> think that maybe we needed you,
> too?

Prejean is taken back.

> PREJEAN
> Oh, Mr. Delacroix. I'm so
> sorry.

The Percys approach.

(CONTINUED)

78 CONTINUED: **78**

>   DELACROIX
> This is Marybeth and Clyde
> Percy, Hope's parents.
>
>   PREJEAN
> Hello. I'm very sorry about
> your daughter.
>
>   CLYDE
> Yeah. So are we. Excuse us.

They leave. Earl remains. People have started to drift back
into the hearing room.

>   DELACROIX
> Listen, Sister, I'm sure you've
> seen a side of Matt Poncelet
> that none of us has seen. I'm
> sure he must be pretty
> sympathetic to you, I'm sure
> he's on his best behavior. But,
> Sister, this is a man that hung
> out in bars with thieves. This
> is an evil man. That scum
> robbed me of my only son, my
> name. My family name dies with
> me. There will be no more
> Delacroixs, Sister.

Henry approaches. Delacroix leaves abruptly.

>   HENRY
> Excuse me for interrupting. The
> Board is back.

79 INT. PARDON BOARD HEARING ROOM. DAY.   **79**

Voices drop and there is a subdued stillness and silence as
Board members take their places.

>   MIRABEAU
> It is the finding of this Board
> that clemency be denied to
> Matthew Poncelet. Execution
> will be carried out as
> scheduled one week hence.

Matt's face registers no emotion. Prejean is distraught.
Hilton's face is ashen.

                                                            (CONTINUED)

79 CONTINUED: **79**

> HILTON
> Don't lose hope, Matt. We've
> still got a judge in the fifth
> circuit federal court that can
> stop it and beyond that there's
> the U.S. Supreme Court and the
> governor. I'll get a private
> meeting with him if it's the
> last thing I do. Don't lose hope.

> MATT
> Looks like you're all I've got,
> Sis. They tell me I can have a
> spiritual adviser of my choice.
> How's about it? Want to ride
> alongside me into the sunset?
> Matt is escorted out by guards.

80 INT. PARDON BOARD BUILDING. DAY.   **80**

Hilton and Prejean walk.

> HILTON
> It means you are with him every
> day for several hours as his
> death nears. On the day of
> execution you are there all
> day. This kind of deal is
> usually done by a priest, a
> chaplain, a Moslem cleric. It's
> a tough job. If you're up to
> it, I say go for it.

> PREJEAN
> Oh boy.

> HILTON
> Sister, I want you to be
> realistic. We got a 1 in 1000
> chance something might go our way.
> It's gonna be a tough road.

Helen sees Delacroix and moves toward him.[20]

> PREJEAN
> Listen Mr. Delacroix, I want
> you to know that I care about
> you and your family and what
> happened to your son.

                                          (CONTINUED)

80 CONTINUED: **80**

She takes out a pen and pad.

> PREJEAN
> Here's my phone number. Please
> call if there's anything I can
> do to help.

> DELACROIX
> Me call you? Think about that,
> Sister. Think about how
> arrogant and self-righteous
> that is. Excuse me.

He leaves. We HOLD on Prejean, stunned.

81 OMITTED   **81**

82 EXT. ST. THOMAS PROJECTS. NIGHT.[21]   **82**

From Prejean's apartment window we see Herbie, the kid that
was shot, hanging out with several teenage boys.

83 INT. PREJEAN'S APARTMENT. NIGHT.[22]   **83**

Helen is on the phone.

> PREJEAN
> There's no one there.

> COLLEEN
> Where?

> PREJEAN
> At the Delacroix.

Prejean puts the phone down on its cradle and comes into
the room.

84 EXT. SLIDELL STREET. DAY.   **84**

Prejean drives. We see Helen, in CLOSE. She is troubled.
The shock radio jock, Purvis Slade rants:

                                              (CONTINUED)

84   CONTINUED: 84

                              SLADE (V.O.)
                    Oh please, don't kill him. He
                    is a child of God, he deserves
                    more, he is reformed, he's a
                    poet. Blah blah blah. Bleeding
                    heart blah blah blah.
                    Attention. All ye folks, ye
                    advocates of killers and child
                    molesters, ye opponents of
                    execution: Ye cannot walk upon
                    the high ground, ye do not have
                    the moral authority to walk
                    there. Ye traverse with scum,
                    and scum is where ye lay.

85   EXT. DELACROIX HOUSE. DAY.   85

Prejean approaches the door cautiously, waits, gathers her
courage and rings the bell. She waits and as she is about
to ring again, the door opens. Earl Delacroix stands,
disheveled, and slightly startled.

                              DELACROIX
                    What do you want?

                              PREJEAN
                    Mr. Delacroix, forgive me for
                    intruding but I haven't been
                    able to get you out of my mind.
                    I've been calling you but there
                    was no answer. Can I talk with
                    you?

A pause as Earl sizes her up.

                              DELACROIX
                    Come in.

86   INT. DELACROIX HOUSE. DAY.   86

As they walk in:

                              PREJEAN
                    Mr. Delacroix, look, I'm
                    really, really sorry for not
                    coming to see you or your wife.
                    I've never been involved with
                    anything like this before.

                                                        (CONTINUED)

86 CONTINUED: **86**

> DELACROIX
> Truth is you're scared.

> PREJEAN
> Yes.

> DELACROIX
> You oughta be scared. Care for
> some coffee?

> PREJEAN
> No thanks.

The house is in disarray. Picture frames lay on their face on a
mantle. There are half-packed boxes around. Someone is moving.

> DELACROIX
> Sister, can I ask you a
> question? Are you a Communist?

> PREJEAN
> (stunned)
> A Communist? No, Mr. Delacroix,
> I am not a Communist.

> DELACROIX
> I didn't think so. That's what
> some people around here are
> saying, with you defending this
> murderer, but I didn't think
> so. Sit down.

She sits. He goes into the kitchen. We look around the room.

> DELACROIX
> Sorry about the mess. My wife
> and I had a big fight. When we
> got back from the pardon board
> hearing she took Walter's
> clothes out of his closet and
> put them in boxes, called
> Goodwill. She says she wants to
> put the past behind her. She's
> not herself.

> PREJEAN
> She must be going through hell.

(CONTINUED)

86 CONTINUED: (2)   86

Delacroix re-enters. He has picked up a picture and hands
it to Prejean. It is a color picture of Walter Delacroix,
young, smiling, full of life.

                    DELACROIX
          When it first happened she
          would have me bring her to
          Walter's grave every morning.
          She wept a river, poor woman,
          whole days, nights, for weeks,
          months. I wish there was some
          way, some key into the past to
          change it, it tears me up. She
          used to be a ball, we would
          have us some times, boy, laugh
          our heads off.

An awkward pause.

                    DELACROIX
          Walter learned to walk on this
          rug here. He busted his chin on
          the arm of this sofa. At that
          kitchen table in there he sat
          with Hope a week before they
          died. When you lose a child all
          the memories get sealed in a
          place. Sealed. Like a shrine.

87 INT. CHAPLAINS OFFICE. DAY.   87

                    FARLEY
          So you have put in a request to
          be the spiritual adviser to
          Matthew Poncelet. Why?

                    PREJEAN
          He asked me.

                    FARLEY
          It's highly irregular.

                    PREJEAN
          Why?

                    FARLEY
          Well, you'd be the first woman
          to do it. This boy is to be

                    (MORE)

                                                    (CONTINUED)

87   CONTINUED: 87

                              FARLEY (CONT'D)
                    executed in five days and is in
                    dire need of redemption. This
                    kind of situation needs an
                    experienced hand.

                              PREJEAN
                    He has asked me, Father.

                              FARLEY
                    These are high stakes, Sister.
                    If you fail, this boy's soul is
                    damned. Are you up to this?

                              PREJEAN
                    Yes, Father.

                              FARLEY
                    You're sure?

                              PREJEAN
                    Yes.

                              FARLEY
                    You can save this boy by
                    getting him to receive the
                    sacraments of the church before
                    he dies. This is your job.
                    Nothing more, nothing less.

88   INT. DEATH ROW. DAY.   88

Outside is another rainy day.

                              MATT
                    I don't want to be buried here.
                    They said they was gonna call
                    my mama and talk to her about
                    the funeral and all the
                    arrangements. You've gotta help
                    me. Can you take care of it? I
                    just don't want my mama mixed
                    up in this. She wouldn't be
                    able to stand it.

                              PREJEAN
                    I'll take care of it, Matt.

A pause.

                                                        (CONTINUED)

88 CONTINUED: **88**

> PREJEAN
> Do you ever read the Bible?

> MATT
> Yes ma'am. I ain't much of a
> Bible reader but I pick it up
> and read it sometimes.

> PREJEAN
> Like W.C. Fields read his
> Bible?

> MATT
> Who?

> PREJEAN
> W.C. Fields used to play this
> drunken character in the
> movies. So he's on his deathbed
> and a friend comes to visit
> him, sees him reading the
> Bible. His friend says, "W.C.
> you don't believe in God. Why
> you reading the Bible?" and
> Fields says, "I'm lookin' for a
> loophole."

Matt smiles.

> MATT
> No, it's not a loophole I'm
> looking for.

Matt is distracted. He looks out the window.

> MATT
> Rain, rain, rain; not a good
> sign.

He sighs.

> MATT
> They already executed one
> black, Tobias, and tonight
> Wayne Purcell -- two blacks.
> It's time for a white; the
> governor is under pressure to
> get a white. And that's me.

(CONTINUED)

88 CONTINUED: (2)   88

Matt gets up and paces, looking for a sign of Wayne
Purcell.

> MATT
> A nigger in the gurney before
> me. I sure hope they clean that
> thing before they put me on it.

A pause.

> PREJEAN
> Was your daddy a racist?

> MATT
> What kind of question is that?

> PREJEAN
> Hatred for people is taught. I
> was wondering who taught you.

> MATT
> I just don't like niggers.

> PREJEAN
> Have you ever known any?

> MATT
> Sure I did. When I was a kid
> they was all around.

> PREJEAN
> All around?

> MATT
> They lived around me.

> PREJEAN
> Did you ever play with any
> black children?

> MATT
> No, but me and my cousin got
> jumped pretty bad once.

> PREJEAN
> What happened?

(CONTINUED)

CONTINUED: (3)

                          MATT
          We was throwin' some rocks at
          'em, and the next day they
          waited their chance and got a
          hold of our bikes and tore 'em
          up.

                          PREJEAN
          Can you blame them?

                          MATT
          No. But listen, slavery's long
          over. They keep harpin' on what
          a bad deal they had.

                          PREJEAN
          Who? The kids that tore up your
          bikes?

                          MATT
          Yeah, them and all of them. I
          can't stand people that make
          themselves out to be victims.

                          PREJEAN
          Victims?

                          MATT
          They all victims.

                          PREJEAN
          I don't know any victims in my
          neighborhood. I know some
          pretty cool people. Hard
          working, decent.

                          MATT
          Well, I know a lot of lazy,
          welfare-taking niggers, sucking
          up tax dollars.

                          PREJEAN
          You sound like a politician.

                          MATT
          What do you mean?

                                          (CONTINUED)

88   CONTINUED: (4)   88

                    PREJEAN
          Have you ever been the object
          of prejudice?

                    MATT
          No.

                    PREJEAN
          What do you think people think
          of death-row inmates?

                    MATT
          I don't know. Why don't you
          tell me?

                    PREJEAN
          They're all monsters.
          Disposable human waste. Good
          for nothings suckin' up tax
          dollars.

                    MATT
          But I ain't a victim. They
          about to kill me and I'm
          innocent. I ain't whining.
          I ain't sitting on a porch
          saying "slavery" and all. I
          like rebels. Like Martin Luther
          King. He led his people,
          marched all the way to D.C.,
          kicked the white man's butt.

                    PREJEAN
          So you respect Martin Luther
          King?

                    MATT
          He put up a fight. He wasn't
          lazy.

                    PREJEAN
          What about lazy whites?

                    MATT
          Don't like 'em.

                                        (CONTINUED)

88 CONTINUED (5)   **88**

> PREJEAN
> So it's lazy people you don't
> like?

> MATT
> Can we talk about something
> else.

89 EXT. ANGOLA PRISON/INT. TRAPP PRISON VEHICLE. DAY.[23]   **89**

Prejean is being driven to the front gate by a guard. This
is NEAL TRAPP. He is in his forties, balding, gray. As they
drive we see a flurry of activity.

> TRAPP
> You gotta stay ahead of these
> guys, don't forget who the fox
> is and who the hen is. In
> training we're told not to
> share anything personal with
> the inmates. It's good advice.

> PREJEAN
> How long have you worked here?

> TRAPP
> Since I was nineteen.

> PREJEAN
> You like it?

> TRAPP
> Hell yeah. It's steady bread.
> Runs in the family, too. I'm
> third generation Angola guard.

They pass a building that seems to be a hub of activity.

> PREJEAN
> What is that?

> TRAPP
> That's the death house; where
> they're going to execute this
> guy Wayne Purcell tonight.
> State hasn't done a lethal
> injection before, everybody's
> kind of nervous. They gettin'
> ready to practice.

90 OMITTED   **90**

91 EXT. ANGOLA PRISON. NIGHT.   **91**

We see protesters and supporters of the death penalty.
People carry signs, e.g., "Teach 'em about Jesus and then
fry 'em." The electronic media is there. Reporters mill
about. Prejean is there with Colleen and the other sisters.

> SUPPORTER
> "Whoever doth shed blood shall
> have his blood shed." Read your
> Bible. It's right there.

The sisters are praying. The supporters of the death
penalty begin a countdown, as if this were New Year's Eve
at midnight. When they reach zero, there is applause from
the supporters, cheers, hoots, catcalls.

92 EXT. ANGOLA PRISON. NIGHT.   **92**

Some time later, the crowd has thinned out. Clyde Percy is
being interviewed.

> CLYDE
> It's the only way we can be sure
> they will never kill again. Life
> without parole, sure, but how many
> prison guards, other prisoners
> will they kill? These are maddogs,
> psychos.

The gates to the prison begin to open. A white prison van
is behind it. Also, a curious thing; Prejean passes the
prison guard, Trapp, and as she passes him she sees tears
in his eyes.

93 EXT. LOUISIANA HIGHWAY./INT. PREJEAN CAR. NIGHT.   **93**

Prejean sits in the backseat next to Sister Colleen. No one
in the car says anything, the silence speaks volumes.
Colleen begins to sing. We see the faces of the other nuns
in the car.[24] Warriors with wounds that have no time to
convalesce. They'll be back at it tomorrow.

> PREJEAN
> How do you plan for a death?

> COLLEEN
> What?

(CONTINUED)

93 CONTINUED: 93

                              PREJEAN
                    I have to make funeral
                    arrangements for Matt. If the
                    courts and the governor turn us
                    down, Matt will be dead in five
                    days. We need a funeral home.
                    And a place to bury him.

                              COLLEEN
                    Maybe our sisters will donate
                    one of their burial plots.

                              PREJEAN
                    And we have to find someone to
                    do the burial service. And
                    clothes. He'll need a suit to
                    be buried in.

                              COLLEEN
                    A suit. What size suit do you
                    think he wears? How tall is he?

                              PREJEAN
                    I think he's kinda big. What
                    size is big? What is it -- big,
                    medium, and petite?

They laugh.

                              PREJEAN
                    I don't know. I've never bought
                    a man's suit before.

                              COLLEEN
                    Won't you be a pretty sight. A
                    nun shopping for a man's suit.

                              PREJEAN
                    I'm out of my league. This is
                    so surreal.

94 INT. PERCY HOUSE. DAY.   94

Prejean, Clyde, and Marybeth sit in comfortable chairs in
the front living room. Hope's graduation picture hangs on
the living room wall. The Percys seem eager to talk.

(CONTINUED)

94   CONTINUED: 94

                           MARYBETH
              Hope had just graduated from
              high school in early May. She
              was to join the Air Force on
              June 15th, the day it happened.
              She almost got out of Slidell.

                           CLYDE
              She was hoping to be stationed
              overseas. She always liked
              traveling, being with people of
              different cultures.

                           MARYBETH
              On June 15th a recruiting
              sergeant was going to meet Hope
              at her apartment and drive her
              to Baton Rouge for induction. I
              had taken her shopping the day
              before to get some things she
              would be needing. You know,
              practical things, new bras with
              plenty of support, dental
              floss, medicine for menstrual
              cramps, stuff like that.

                           CLYDE
              At about five in the evening,
              Hope left to go to work at
              Corey's where she waitressed.
              After work she had a date with
              Walter.

                           MARYBETH
              As she was leaving I noticed
              that part of her hem was coming
              out of her skirt. She was in
              such a hurry I pinned it for
              her with one of those tiny
              safety pins, and she was gone,
              out the door.

95   INT. COURT ROOM. DAY - FLASHBACK.   95

We are close on the skirt in a cellophane bag. On the bag
it says: State's Exhibit 10. We pull out to see the bag in
the hand of Gilardi.

                                              (CONTINUED)

95 CONTINUED: 95

> MARYBETH
> Yes, that's it.

We see the safety pin. The skirt is placed down on a table
next to a purse, a beige blouse, a driver's license, a
ring, a class pin, a watch with a blue face.

> MARYBETH (V.O.)
> You don't know when you see
> your child leave through a door
> that you are never going to see
> her alive again. If I had
> known, I would have told her
> how much I loved her.

96 INT. PERCY HOUSE. DAY. 96

> MARYBETH
> My last words to her -- the
> last she ever heard from me --
> was about the hem of a skirt.

> CLYDE
> The next morning we waited for
> Hope to come through her door;
> the big day! Our baby was
> leaving home.

97 INT. HOPE'S BEDROOM (1988). DAY - FLASHBACK. 97

The door opens. Clyde and Marybeth enter.

> MARYBETH(V.O.)
> It was empty. Her bed was still
> neatly made.

We are CLOSE on Marybeth and Clyde.

98 INT. PERCY HOUSE. DAY. 98

We are CLOSE on Helen.

> MARYBETH
> I called the Delacroixs. It was
> strange that she did not call.
> She would always telephone me
> and tell me where she was.

(CONTINUED)

98   CONTINUED: 98

                              CLYDE
                    Our hearts sank when the
                    Delacroixs said Walter didn't
                    come home either. And for a
                    brief moment it crossed our
                    minds that maybe they had run
                    off and gotten married or
                    something.

                              MARYBETH
                    But we knew Hope was too
                    sensible a girl to do a thing
                    like that.

                              CLYDE
                    I went to the police, filed a
                    missing persons report. Three
                    days passed. The sheriff's
                    office finally formed a search
                    party. I went with them.

                              MARYBETH
                    They looked all day. Walked for
                    miles. Nothing.

99   EXT. LOUISIANA WOODS (1988). DAY - FLASHBACK.   99

      We see a search party looking through the woods, dogs
      sniffing. Clyde is with them.

                              CLYDE (V.O.)
                    On Thursday, June 20th some
                    kids walking near Flank's Cove
                    found a purse, clothes, and a
                    wallet and handed them over to
                    the police. A friend of ours
                    called us to tell us that they
                    had heard that some of Hope's
                    things had been found.

100   INT. PERCY HOUSE. DAY.   100

      We are CLOSE on a picture of Hope.

                                                          (CONTINUED)

100   CONTINUED: 100

                          MARYBETH
           We got that information from
           our own resources, not from the
           police. They never called up.
           We called them.

                          CLYDE
           They found their bodies on
           Friday, six days after her
           disappearance.

101   EXT. FLANK'S COVE (1988). TWILIGHT - FLASHBACK.   101

Men in masks surround the pale, stiff body of Hope Percy.

102   INT. PERCY HOUSE. DAY.   102

                          MARYBETH
           My daughter's body was nude,
           supine, legs spread-eagled.
           The coroner's report said her
           vagina was all tore up. At
           first they couldn't find the
           class pin she was wearing
           because it was embedded so deep
           from the stabbing. She had been
           so proud of that pin. She wore
           it all the time. It said:
           "Class of '88,' Making a
           Difference."

                          CLYDE
           The police wouldn't let us come
            to the morgue to identify the
           body, said it would be too
           traumatic.

                          MARYBETH
           But I couldn't bear the thought
           of the body being buried
           forever without being
           absolutely, positively sure
           without a doubt that it was
           Hope. What if, because of the
           decomposition and the clothes
           being nearby, they only thought
           it was Hope? I had to be sure.
           I called my brother in Metaire,
           a dentist, and I asked him to
           go to the funeral home and make
           an ID from dental records.

                                       (CONTINUED)

CONTINUED:102

> CLYDE
> Marybeth's brother was pretty
> tore up when he came back from
> the funeral home. Before he
> reached his hand into that bag
> with all the lime in it and
> fished out Hope's jaw, he said
> he had always been against the
> death penalty. But, boy, after
> that, he was for it.

> MARYBETH
> I knew it had to be Hope,
> that's what my mind told me,
> but I just had to be sure.

EMILY, the fourteen-year-old daughter of Clyde and
Marybeth, dashes into living room. She leans close to her
mother and whispers something.

> MARYBETH
> Emily, this is Sister Prejean.

> EMILY
> Hello.

> PREJEAN
> Nice to meet you, Emily.

> EMILY
> OK.

She turns the TV on. Inside, darkness has been slowly
seeping into the room. Marybeth gets up and turns on a
lamp.

> MARYBETH
> Let's go to the kitchen and
> I'll make us some coffee.

103INT. COURTHOUSE HALLWAY. DAY - FLASHBACK.103

> CLYDE (V.O.)
> Poncelet and I met face to face
> in the hallway during the
> trial.

We see Matt Poncelet, in handcuffs, being led by sheriff's
deputies.

(CONTINUED)

103 CONTINUED: 103

                         MATT
              I ain't going to the chair,
              daddy.

                         CLYDE
              You're going to fry and I'm
              going to watch you sizzle.

104 INT. PERCY KITCHEN. DAY.   104

Marybeth is pouring coffee into cups.

                         CLYDE
              A policeman was right near me.
              I could've taken his gun and
              shot him, right there. I
              could've killed him that day. I
              should have. I'd be a happier
              man today.

There is a pause.

                         MARYBETH
              So what made you change your
              mind?

                         PREJEAN
              Change my mind?

                         MARYBETH
              What made you come around to
              our side?

                         PREJEAN
              I'm...I...I wanted to come to
              see if I could help you. But
              I... I haven't...Mr. Poncelet
              asked me to be his spiritual
              adviser. I'm going to be with
              him when he dies.

                         CLYDE
              I thought you'd changed your
              mind. I thought that's why you
              were here.

                         PREJEAN
              No. I uh...

(CONTINUED)

104   CONTINUED: 104

A Pause

                         MARYBETH
          How can you...come here?

                         CLYDE
          How can you go there? How can
          you sit with that scum?

                         PREJEAN
          I try to follow the example of
          Jesus, that every person is
          worth more than his worst act.

                         CLYDE
          This is not a person. This is
          an animal. No, I take that
          back. Animals don't rape and
          kill their own kind. Matt
          Poncelet is God's mistake.
          And you hold the poor
          murderer's hand? You're going
          to comfort him when he dies? No
          one was there to comfort Hope
          when those two animals put her
          face down in the wet grass in
          those woods.

                         PREJEAN
          I've never done this before,
          Mr. Percy. I'm trying to get
          him to take responsibility for
          what he did.

                         MARYBETH
          Does he admit to what he did?
          Is he sorry?

                         PREJEAN
          He says he didn't kill anybody.

                         CLYDE
          Sister, you're in waters over
          your head. I'm trying to be
          respectful because my parents
          taught me to always respect the
          religious, but I think you need
          to leave this house.

                                          (CONTINUED)

104 CONTINUED: (2)   **104**

> MARYBETH
> You don't know what it is to
> carry a child in your womb and
> give birth and get up with a
> sick child in the middle of the
> night. You say your prayers and
> get a good night's sleep, don't
> you?

> PREJEAN
> I'm so sorry about your
> daughter.

> CLYDE
> If you are sorry and if you
> care about us, you'll want to
> see justice done for our
> murdered child. But you can't
> have it both ways. You can't
> befriend this murderer and be
> our friend, too.

> MARYBETH
> You've brought the enemy into
> this house, Sister. You'd
> better go.

As she goes.

> PREJEAN
> I'm sorry. I'm sorry.[25] I've
> only added to your pain.

105 EXT. CAUSEWAY/INT. PREJEAN CAR. DAY.   **105**

Music. Prejean drives, tears in her eyes, overcome by the
mixed messages and conflicting emotions she is feeling.

106 INT. PRISON. DAY.   **106**

Matt is being interviewed.

> MATT
> I come from a good family. My
> family's not to blame for
> nothin'. I had two families,
> both of them I love and would
> die for.

                                                        (CONTINUED)

106 CONTINUED: 106

                         REPORTER
               Your other family is?

                         MATT
               The family of man, of men in
               jail. My white family, the
               Aryan Brotherhood.

                         REPORTER
               You are a white supremacist, a
               follower of Hitler?

                         MATT
               Hitler was a leader. I admire
               that he got things done. Like
               Castro. He got things done,
               man. Now maybe Hitler went a
               little overboard with some of
               his killin' but he was on the
               right track about Aryans being
               the master race.

                         REPORTER
               The right track? The murder of
               six million Jews?

107 INT. PREJEAN APARTMENT. NIGHT.   107

Prejean and other nuns watch Matt Poncelet on the
television.

                         MATT (ON TV)
               That hasn't been proven.

The phone rings.

                         PREJEAN
               Man, what am I doing with this
               guy? I must be nuts.

Prejean picks it up.

                         HILTON (V.O.)
               We need you to come in for a
               strategy meeting.

                                          (CONTINUED)

107 CONTINUED: 107

                              MATT (ON TV)
                    Your government's been doing
                    plenty of evil things
                    themselves, and you're paying
                    for it; trying to assassinate
                    political enemies like Castro,
                    Allende, the Sandinistas. The
                    government shouldn't be given
                    power to execute nobody.
                    They're too corrupt, man.

108 INT. HILTON BARBER'S OFFICE. DAY.   108

     Prejean, Hilton, and his associates, Henry and NELLIE, sit
     around a table. Everybody looks pretty ragged. Prejean has
     a bad cough from breathing in all the cigarette smoke. She
     sits by a window, distracted. Outside we see some slackers
     hanging out.

                              NELLIE
                    In an interview with the Times-
                    Picayune, Poncelet says that if
                    he had it to do all over again
                    he would "do something useful
                    like join a terrorist group and
                    bomb government buildings."
                    We've got to get him off this
                    political prisoner kick.

                              HILTON
                    Henry, how close are we on the
                    Supreme Court docket?

                              HENRY
                    A couple of days.

                              HILTON
                    We don't have a couple of days.

                              HENRY
                    Well we don't have the staff,
                    Hilton.

                              HILTON
                    You've had it for three days.
                    Where were you yesterday
                    anyway?

                                                      (CONTINUED)

108 CONTINUED: **108**

> HENRY
> I had to take my kid to the
> dentist.

> HILTON
> A man is going to die on death
> row....

> HENRY
> ...and my kid needed her daddy
> to hold her hand, yes, Hilton.
> If you don't like it find some
> other lawyer to volunteer his
> time.

We see Prejean, thinking of something else, looking out the
window, far away from the room.

AA109 INT. DEATH HOUSE DAY. **AA109**

> PREJEAN
> People are reading these
> interviews thinking you're some
> kind of nut, admiring Hitler,
> saying you'd like to come back
> as a terrorist and bomb people.

> MATT
> Not the people, just the
> buildings. I didn't say I'd
> bomb the people.

> PREJEAN
> How can you bomb a buildin'
> without hurting somebody?

> MATT
> I don't have any love for the
> U.S. government is all.

> PREJEAN
> You're a fool. Don't you see
> how easy you're making it for
> them to kill you? You're coming
> off as a crazed animal, a Nazi
> terrorist maddog, someone
> that's not even human that
> deserves to die.

(CONTINUED)

                      MATT
Do you think that?

                    PREJEAN
You're making it very difficult
for us to help you.

                      MATT
Well you can leave.

Pause.

                    PREJEAN
I'm not going to do that.

Pause.

                    PREJEAN
Do you ever think about those
kids?

                      MATT
It's terrible what happened to
those kids.

                    PREJEAN
Especially since it didn't have
to happen. And the parents. Do
you and Vitello ever think
about what you did to those
parents' lives?

                      MATT
It's hard, ma'am, to be having
much sympathy for the parents
when, here, they're trying to
kill me.

                    PREJEAN
Think about it. Their kids
shot, stabbed, and left to die
in the woods. Alone. What if
someone did that to your mama?
You're little brother? What
would you do to them?

                      MATT
Kill 'em. I sure as hell would
want to kill 'em.

                            (CONTINUED)

AA109 CONTINUED: (2)   AA109

A pause.

                        MATT
          I want to take a lie detector
          test.

                        PREJEAN
          What?

                        MATT
          A lie detector test. It ain't
          gonna change any of these guys
          minds, but I would like my mama
          to know the truth. I want her
          to know I didn't kill those
          kids.

A109 INT. STAIRWELL. NIGHT.   A109

Prejean walks up the stairs to her apartment.

109   INT. PREJEAN APARTMENT/STAIRWELL. NIGHT.   109

Prejean enters the front door. Colleen is there and so are
a couple of kids. When the kids see her they get up.

                        KID #1
          Bye sister. We gotta go.

                        PREJEAN
          How you doin' Sally?

                        KID #1
          I'm OK. Let's go, Ro.

The two kids leave.

                        COLLEEN
          There's talk in the
          neighborhood. Someone read some
          of Poncelet's racist comments.
          Your name was in the article.

                        PREJEAN
          Oh, Lord.

                                              (CONTINUED)

> COLLEEN
> They're also wondering where
> you've been at the learning
> center. Think you care more
> about him than your classes.

> PREJEAN
> Oh, man. I'm so sorry, Colleen.

> COLLEEN
> It's alright. I still love you.
> I just thought you should know.

A pause. Colleen takes a man's suit out of the closet.

> COLLEEN
> Got this at Goodwill. I talked
> to Bishop Norwich. He said he
> would say the funeral mass. The
> leaders of the congregation
> have met and we can use one of
> our own burial plots. I also
> found a funeral home willing to
> donate their services.

Prejean holds the suit.

> COLLEEN
> Guess who Matt Poncelet's gonna
> be buried next to?

> PREJEAN
> Who was the last to die?

> COLLEEN
> Sister Celestine.

Helen bursts out laughing.

> PREJEAN
> Oh, Lord.

> COLLEEN
> Remember when that sweet little
> girl came to the convent after
> her wedding to introduce her
> husband to us?

                                        (CONTINUED)

109 CONTINUED: (2)   109

                                    PREJEAN
                    And Celestine says, "I'm glad I
                    don't have to share my bed with any
                    man."

                                    COLLEEN
                    She loved her celibacy so much.

                                    PREJEAN
                    Now she'll have a man next to
                    her forever.

They laugh. Then:

                                    COLLEEN
                    How'd we ever get involved with
                    this stuff anyway?

A110 INT. VICTIMS' RIGHTS MEETING ROOM. NIGHT   A110
      (OLD 120 - ALREADY SHOT)

Prejean sits next to Earl Delacroix. They are at a victims'
support group meeting. We stay on a TWO SHOT of them as we
hear overlapping voices.

                                    VOICE
                    My little twelve-year-old daughter
                    was stabbed to death in our back
                    yard by my son's best friend. He
                    had spent the night at our house
                    and gone to church with us that
                    very morning. Her little skiing
                    outfit is still in the closet. I
                    can't give it away.

The CAMERA MOVES IN toward Prejean.

                                    VOICE
                    When our child was killed, it
                    took over a week to find her
                    body. The D.A.'s office treated
                    us like we were the criminals.
                    Whenever we telephoned to find
                    out what was happening, they
                    brushed us off. They wouldn't
                    tell us when the trial was
                    happening. They wouldn't tell
                    us anything.

                                                        (CONTINUED)

Now we are TIGHT on Prejean.

>   VOICE
>   Our daughter was killed by her
>   ex-husband in our front yard
>   with her children watching.
>   Bang! Bang! Bang! He shot her,
>   then himself right there on the
>   front lawn....

>   VOICE
>   Recently, my wife and I went to
>   the sheriff's office to apply
>   for victim compensation funds.
>   A deputy rifled through a few
>   drawers and said, "Don't know
>   nothin' about these funds. Why
>   don't ya'll write to Ann
>   Landers? She helps people."

Now we see at the table, Earl Delacroix.

>   DELACROIX
>   Friends were supportive at
>   first, at the time our son was
>   killed, but now they avoid us.
>   They don't know what to say,
>   what to do. If you bring up
>   your child's death, they change
>   the subject. I keep getting the
>   feeling that they think I
>   should be able to put his death
>   behind me by now and get on
>   with my life. People have no
>   idea what you go through when
>   something like this happens to
>   you.

We see Prejean, in TIGHT, moved.

>   DELACROIX
>   My wife and I are getting a
>   separation.[26] We just have
>   different ways of dealing with
>   our son's death. "Until death
>   do us part."

                                              (CONTINUED)

A110 CONTINUED: (2)   **A110**

We start TIGHT on Prejean. The CAMERA BEGINS to pull back.
Again we hear an overlapping of voices:

> VOICE
> My daughter's killer can
> possibly get out on parole in
> another year. He's only served
> six years. I can't bear the
> thought that he would be out a
> free man and she's buried in
> the ground and dead forever.
> Six years is nothing. This
> isn't justice.

As we PULL OUT we see Earl Delacroix, once again next to
Prejean. She has her arm around him in support. He is
weeping.

> VOICE
> I just lost my job. Just
> couldn't pull it together. I'd
> be staring out of the window
> and couldn't concentrate. They
> let me go last week.

B110 EXT. SCHOOL. NIGHT.(OLD 121 - ALREADY SHOT)   **B110**

The meeting over, Prejean walks with Delacroix in the
parking lot.

> DELACROIX
> We're nothing special. Most
> folks that lose a kid split up.
> About 70 percent. I just wish I
> could laugh, find something
> funny.

> PREJEAN
> Thanks for having me, Mr. Delacroix.
> All this sorrow in one room; I
> thought my heart would break.

> DELACROIX
> You take care, Sister.

> PREJEAN
> Drive safely.

110 OMITTED
                                                               110

111 OMITTED   **111**

112 EXT. ANGOLA PRISON. DAY.   **112**

Prejean travels in a prison van with Sgt. Trapp on the way
to the death house. We see, from her POV, a prison
cemetery; simple white crosses without names. Prisoners
going to work in the fields guarded by armed men on
horseback. Intercut with this we see images of the murder.

113 INT. DEATH HOUSE ENTRANCE AREA. DAY.   **113**

Trapp brings Prejean in.

                         GUARD
                Empty your pockets.

He runs a metal detector over her body. A GUARD sits on a
metal folding chair. He has a fresh-scrubbed baby face and
wears a .357 Magnum strapped to his side.

114 OMITTED[27]   **114**

A115 INT. DEATH HOUSE. DAY.   **A115**

                         MATT
                Like my new digs? I'm pretty
                special, huh? Got this place
                all to myself. Got eight guys
                guarding me. One dude checks me
                every fifteen minutes to see if
                I've killed myself. Suicide
                watch. Never had so many people
                care about how I was doin.

                         PREJEAN
                When did you come out here?

                         MATT
                Last night. Late. Didn't get a chance
                to say goodbye to the guys on the
                row. Most of them were sleeping. Did
                you get me that lie detector test?

                         PREJEAN
                I made some calls. No luck yet.

                                        (CONTINUED)

> MATT
>
> So this is the end. The death house
> vacation. Three days of quiet. Plenty
> of time to read my Bible, eh Sister?
> Look for a loophole.

Pause.

> PREJEAN
>
> Did you read anything in that
> bible about Jesus?

> MATT
>
> Holy man, did good, in heaven,
> praise Jesus.

> PREJEAN
>
> There's passages in there about
> the suffering of Jesus when he
> was alone and facing death that
> you might find interesting.

> MATT
>
> Me and Jesus had a different
> way of dealing with things. He
> was one of those turn the other
> cheek guys.

> PREJEAN
>
> Takes a lot of strength to turn
> the other cheek, Matt. You say
> you like rebels. What do you
> think Jesus was?

> MATT
>
> He wasn't no rebel?

> PREJEAN
>
> Sure he was. He was a dangerous
> man.

> MATT
>
> What's so dangerous about love
> your brother?

(CONTINUED)

A115   CONTINUED: (2)   **A115**

>   PREJEAN
>   His love changed things, Matt.
>   People that nobody cared about
>   prostitutes, beggars, the poor,
>   finally had someone that
>   respected them, loved them,
>   made them realize their own
>   worth. They had dignity and
>   were becoming powerful, and
>   that made the guys at the top
>   so nervous they went and killed
>   Jesus.

>   MATT
>   Kinda like me, huh?

>   PREJEAN
>   No, Matt. Not at all like you.
>   Not at all. He created a better
>   world. He changed it with his
>   love. You stood by and watched
>   while two kids were killed.

115   EXT. DEATH HOUSE/BENCH. DAY.   **115**

Prejean is taking a break, getting some air. Sgt. Trapp,
approaches her.

>   TRAPP
>   Sister Helen, Chaplain Farley
>   called. He's at the gate. He'll
>   be right here.

>   PREJEAN
>   Thanks, Sgt. Trapp.

Trapp delays at the door, as if he wants to say
something.

>   PREJEAN
>   I saw you outside the gates the
>   night of Purcell's execution.

>   TRAPP
>   Yes.

>   PREJEAN
>   You seemed upset.

                                                    (CONTINUED)

CONTINUED:

                              TRAPP
              Upset? No.

                              PREJEAN
              Were you inside the room when
              they did it?

                              TRAPP
              I'm on the strap-down team.
              I'm on the left leg. That's my
              job. The left leg. We take the
              prisoner from his cell into the
              execution chamber.

                              PREJEAN
              Wow. That's gotta be a tough.

                              TRAPP
              It was...hard. I got home that
              night and couldn't sleep. Just
              sat in the chair all night.

                              PREJEAN
              I think this thing must affect
              everybody that sees it, whether
              they're for it or against it.

                              TRAPP
              Well, it's part of the job,
              ma'am, Sister. These people get
              what's comin' to 'em.

       Farley pulls up in a prison van.

                              FARLEY
              Trying to convert Sgt. Trapp to
              your cause? I'm sorry I'm late.

116   INT. DEATH HOUSE OFFICE. DAY.   116

       Farley tidies his desk as he talks.

                              FARLEY
              It's very easy for someone to
              come in from outside and make a
              rash judgment on procedure.
              What may appear on the surface
              to be irrational or unnecessary
              proves upon examination to have
              solid reasoning and experience
              behind it.

                                                                (CONTINUED)

>   PREJEAN
> Father, all I'm asking is to
> play a hymn for Matt before his
> execution.

>   FARLEY
> And experience tells us that
> music stirs up emotion, emotion
> that may produce an unexpected
> reaction in the inmate.

>   PREJEAN
> Would you mind if I ask the
> warden for his opinion?

>   FARLEY
> I would discourage it, but you
> may, if you like.

>   PREJEAN
> Well thank you for your time,
> Father.

She stands.

>   FARLEY
> I understand you were
> protesting outside the gates
> during the last execution.

>   PREJEAN
> Yes.

>   FARLEY
> Are you familiar with the Old
> Testament, "Thou shalt not kill
> but if thou shed the blood of
> man by man shall your blood be
> shed"?

>   PREJEAN
> Yes. But in the New Testament
> Jesus speaks of grace and
> reconciliation.

                                    (CONTINUED)

116   CONTINUED: (2)   116

                         FARLEY
              Reconciliation is achieved by
              accepting God's love. Poncelet
              has to understand that Jesus
              died for his sins if his soul
              is to live an eternal life. The
              politics of the death penalty
              are not what's important here.
              I certainly hope you're not
              encouraging him to reject
              authority. Look at Romans "Let
              every person be subordinate to
              the higher authorities, for
              there is no authority except
              from God and those who oppose
              it will bring judgment upon
              themselves."

Prejean begins to sway and SHE FAINTS.

117   INT. PRISON HOSPITAL CORRIDOR. DAY.   117

From Prejean's POV we see a nurse, Farley, and CAPTAIN
BELIVEAU hovering above her.

                         NURSE
              What is it? What happened?

                         FARLEY
              She collapsed in my office. I
              think it may be her heart.

                         BELIVEAU
              She's having a heart attack.

                         PREJEAN
              I'm OK. I think I just fainted.

                         BELIVEAU
              You just stay right there young
              lady.

                         PREJEAN
              I haven't eaten anything. I'm
              sure I'm OK.

118   INT. PRISON HOSPITAL. DAY.   **118**

The nurse is monitoring an EKG.

                         PREJEAN
               I told Matt I'd be back. Can
               you tell him what happened?

                         NURSE
               We'll do that when we're
               finished here.

                         PREJEAN
               No. I gotta get word to him.

The nurse looks at the EKG monitor.

                         BELIVEAU
               I'll take care of it, Sister.

                         NURSE
               Well good news, this isn't a
               heart attack.

                         PREJEAN
               I'm just hungry. They have this rule
               you're not allowed to eat in the
               death house. They must think we're
               ferns and can feed off the air.

The nurse begins to detach the EKG.

                         PREJEAN
               Is this machine used after an
               execution?

                         NURSE
               Yes ma'am. We just have to be
               official about the whole thing.
               Thank God we're off the electric
               chair. Smell of burnt flesh and all.
               It's a little easier to take, the
               needle. Part of the job, you know.
               Let's get you up and get some food
               in your stomach.

                         PREJEAN
               Who puts the needle in?

                                        (CONTINUED)

118 CONTINUED: **118**

                              NURSE
                    That's private information.

                              PREJEAN
                    Is it you?

                              NURSE
                    We are not allowed to disclose
                    any specifics regarding the
                    execution procedure.

                              BELIVEAU
                    C'mon Sister, we'll get you a
                    tray of food and then send you
                    home.

                              PREJEAN
                    No I've got to get back to
                    Matt.

                              BELIVEAU
                    Sorry Sister, Warden's orders.
                    You're through for the day.

A119   EXT. PREJEAN'S MOTHER'S HOME. DAY.(OLD A122 - ALREADY SHOT)**A119**

Prejean is on the front porch. She holds the suit.[28]

                              PREJEAN
                    Mama?

Prejean's mother appears from the side of the house.

                              MOTHER
                    Helen? Hi, sweetie.

                              PREJEAN
                    I'm going to need to stay here
                    for a couple of days. Is that
                    alright?

                              MOTHER
                    Of course.

                              PREJEAN
                    It's such a long drive to
                    Angola from New Orleans.

                                              (CONTINUED)

A119   CONTINUED: A119

                              MOTHER
                    Well, if it takes me being
                    closer to a prison to get you
                    here, I'll take it.

She sees the suit.

                              MOTHER
                    Is that for me? It's not quite
                    my color.

Helen laughs, then sits, overcome.

                              PREJEAN
                    It's a lost cause, mama. I'm
                    wasting my time.

                              MOTHER
                    With your criminal?

                              PREJEAN
                    There's so many people
                    grieving. He's caused so much
                    pain.

A pause.

                              MOTHER
                    Maybe you're looking for a way
                    to love Judas, for a love so
                    big that it takes in the evil.

                              PREJEAN
                    I don't know if I can do it,
                    mama.

                              MOTHER
                    Annunciations are common.
                    Incarnations are rare. You do
                    your best, Helen. That's all
                    God asks.

119   OMITTED   119

120   OMITTED   120

121   OMITTED   121

122   INT. WARDEN HARTMAN'S OFFICE, ANGOLA PRISON. DAY.[29]   122

Prejean talks with WARDEN HARTMAN, a short, stocky man in
his early 60s with a square face and a thick gray mustache.
He is smoking a cigar. Conspicuously present on his desk is
a small cassette player that plays the hymn Prejean wants
to play for Matt.

                    HARTMAN
          It's nice enough.

He turns the volume down. It continues to play softly.

                    HARTMAN
          I've been hearing some
          disturbing things about you.

                    PREJEAN
          Such as?

                    HARTMAN
          That you're too emotionally
          involved with Matthew Poncelet
          and unable to fulfill your
          function as spiritual adviser.

                    PREJEAN
          What gives you that idea?

                    HARTMAN
          You fainted in the death house
          and caused a lot of commotion
          for my personnel.

                    PREJEAN
          I fainted out of hunger not
          emotion.

                    HARTMAN
          As warden, one of my major
          responsibilities in this
          execution process is seeing to
          it that condemned inmates get
          good spiritual counsel and a
          chance to get straight with God
          before they die. This man
          Farley is perfectly capable of
          doing that.

                              (CONTINUED)

122 CONTINUED: **122**

                              PREJEAN
                Matt doesn't trust Chaplain
                Farley, and he has the right to
                choose his own spiritual
                counsel, doesn't he?

                              HARTMAN
                Yes.

                              PREJEAN
                It's guaranteed in the
                Constitution, isn't it?

                              HARTMAN
                Yes, it is. But according to
                the Constitution we can bar a
                spiritual adviser from the
                prison security.

                              PREJEAN
                A threat?

                              HARTMAN
                You were with some protesters
                outside the prison during the
                last execution.

                              PREJEAN
                C'mon now I was singing "Cum-
                ba-ai." You may not like having
                me around but you know I'm not
                a threat to prison security.

A pause.

                              PREJEAN
                Warden, this man's going to die
                tommorrow. Doesn't he have a
                right to some solace?

As she says this, he is looking at her and listening, taking
long, slow puffs on his cigar. The hymn ends. There is a pause.

                              HARTMAN
                The hymn is nice. But it'll
                stir up emotion. I can't let
                you play it for Mr. Poncelet.
                As far as the other thing, I
                don't want to get into a debate
                about the Constitution. You can
                continue to see him.

                                                    (CONTINUED)

122   CONTINUED: (2)   122

                              PREJEAN
               Thank you.

                              HARTMAN
               Is his family gonna be there
               tomorrow?

                              PREJEAN
               Yes sir.

                              HARTMAN
               It's important that they are
               there for him.

                              PREJEAN
               And you Warden, you'll be
               there, too?

                              HARTMAN
               Yes ma'am, all day and all night.

       A pause.

                              HARTMAN
               Sister, no one is doing
               handstands about this execution.
               It comes with the job.

123   INT. DEATH HOUSE. DAY.   123

       Entering Angola, Prejean hears the television near Matt's
       cell. A baseball game is on. As she approaches the visitor
       door, she sees that the GUARD stationed to watch Matt has
       moved down closer to the TV to catch a critical play. A
       moment of silence, a play, the two men cheer. Then the
       GUARD moves back to the end of the tier and resumes his
       position. Matt is anxious.

                              MATT
               Where'd you go yesterday?

                              PREJEAN
               They wouldn't let me come back.

                              MATT
               Are you all right?

                                                    (CONTINUED)

123   CONTINUED: **123**

                          PREJEAN
          I'm fine. Just a lot of
          commotion for nothing.

                          MATT
          I kept asking them here what
          happened, but they wouldn't tell
          me nothin'. I thought you had a
          heart attack. I thought I was
          gonna have to go through this by
          myself.

                          PREJEAN
          I'm sorry, Matt. I tried to get
          back. They wouldn't let me.

A pause.

                          PREJEAN
          So the Marlboro Man doesn't
          want to ride into the sunset
          all tough and alone.

No response.

                          MATT
          When they took me away
          yesterday they wouldn't tell me
          why. Took me into a room.
          Started measuring me. Weighed
          me. I think they were trying to
          see how big a coffin I needed.
          When I got back you were gone.
          Spent all day alone.

A pause.

                          MATT
          You ever get lonely?

                          PREJEAN
          Yeah. I do. Sometimes on Sunday
          afternoons, when I smell the
          smoke in the neighborhood from
          family barbecues, hear those
          kids laughing, I sit there in
          my room and feel like a fool.

                                                    (CONTINUED)

                        MATT
What I miss most being here are the
women and just bein' in the
bars and listenin' to music and
dancin' till three or four in the
morning. And I'm not goin' to lie
to you, ma'am, I believed in doing
it. Me and my lady friends we'd get
us a blanket and a bottle or a
little weed and go into the woods
and do it.

                        PREJEAN
Well, Matt, let's face it. If I
had a husband and a family,
chances are I'd be with them
this afternoon, instead of
visiting with you.

                        MATT
True. Glad you're here ma'am.

Matt lights a cigarette.

                        PREJEAN
Those things'll kill you, you know.

Matt laughs. Then suddenly:

                        MATT
They're not going to break me.
I just pray God holds up my
legs tomorrow to make that last
walk. It's the waiting, it's
the countdown that gets you.

                        PREJEAN
We should know about the federal
appeal real soon, and Hilton and I
have an appointment to see the
governor this evening.

                        MATT
The governor. Fat chance in
hell he'll do anything. Risk
his political butt for me?

A pause.

(CONTINUED)

                    MATT
          I shouldn't have said all those
          things about Hitler and being a
          terrorist, all that stuff. It
          was stupid.

                    PREJEAN
          Hartman told me there would be
          no more media interviews.

                    MATT
          Just as well. Shut my stupid
          mouth up.

                    PREJEAN
          I was able to arrange a
          polygraph for tomorrow morning.

                    MATT
          Alright. Good news.

                    PREJEAN
          Now, the man that runs the
          polygraph test has serious
          doubts that they'll get an
          accurate reading of the truth.

                    MATT
          Why?

                    PREJEAN
          Because tomorrow is the day of
          your execution and you're bound
          to be under stress, and the
          test often mistakes stress for
          dishonesty.

                    MATT
          Not a problem. I'm home free.

                    PREJEAN
          Have you been reading your
          bible?

                                          (CONTINUED)

123   CONTINUED: (4)   123

                              MATT
              I tried last night, but reading
              makes me want to sleep. I'm
              trying to stay conscious as
              much as possible. Look, I
              appreciate all the efforts to
              save me, but me and God have
              squared things away. I know
              Jesus died for us on the cross
              and will take care of me
              when I appear before God on
              judgment day.

                              PREJEAN
              You know, Matt, redemption
              isn't some kind of free ticket
              admission that you get because
              Jesus paid the price. You need
              to participate in your own
              redemption. You've got some
              work to do. You may want to
              check out some words of Jesus
              that might have some meaning
              for you: "You shall know the
              truth and the truth will make
              you free." It's in the Gospel
              of John, chapter 8.

                              MATT
              I'll do that. I'll check it
              out. The truth will set you
              free. I like that. I pass that
              lie detector test and I'm home
              free.

                              PREJEAN
              Matt, if you do die, as your
              friend, I want to help you to
              die with dignity, and you can't
              do that, the way I see it,
              until you own up to the part
              you played in Walter and Hope's
              death.

We HOLD on Matt.

124 INT. STATE HOUSE. DUSK.   124

Hilton, Prejean, and Bishop Norwich walk down a corridor,
following a GUIDE.[30]

                          PREJEAN
              Hilton, this is Bishop Norwich.

                          HILTON
              Pleasure, Bishop.

                          NORWICH
              Hello.

                          HILTON
              Now listen, from what I know of
              Benedict, he's a reluctant
              supporter of capital
              punishment. He has the power to
              save this man's life by
              commuting the sentence or
              granting a reprieve. The last
              vestige of the right of kings.
              The trick on this is to appeal
              to him on a personal level,
              without a lot of fanfare.
              That's why I've requested a
              private meeting.

They are directed into a large room where there are TV
cameras, bright lights, reporters and a large conference
table.

                          PREJEAN
              What is happening?

                          HILTON
              I don't know. I can't imagine
              this is for us.

The guide shows the three to seats at the conference table.
The governor is in mid-sentence.

                          FREDERICKS
              ...with the Catholic Bishops
              clearing up a little
              misunderstanding about my
              position on the resurrection of
              Christ. Unfortunately I was
              misquoted on the subject by a
              member of your esteemed
              profession, and I am happy to
              say that our meeting this
              morning has cleared up this
              matter of the resurrection.

                                        (CONTINUED)

124   CONTINUED: 124

The PRESS chuckles.

                    FREDERICKS
             Now, tomorrow, as you know, the
             State of Louisiana will put to
             death Matthew Poncelet, and
             today I have invited a couple
             of people here to talk to us
             about this case. Who will go
             first?

                    HILTON
             Yes well, uh... Matt Poncelet
             had inadequate counsel....

125   DISSOLVE TO:[31]   125

                BISHOP NORWICH
             ...the death penalty is a
             simplistic solution to a
             complex moral issue; executions
             signal to society that violence
             is an acceptable way of dealing
             with human problems....

126   DISSOLVE TO: 126

                BISHOP NORWICH
             ...he could be a productive
             prisoner in Angola, serving a
             life sentence. What will be
             accomplished by killing him?

127   DISSOLVE TO: 127

                    FREDERICKS
             But you must understand, I'm
             the governor and represent the
             state and must carry out the
             laws and must submerge my own
             personal views to carry out the
             expressed will of the people.
             And I'm hesitant to express my
             own views on the subject,
             because it can end up like this
             resurrection controversy.

                                 (CONTINUED)

127   CONTINUED: 127

Laughter.

                    FREDERICKS
          Yes, I'll look carefully at the
          case, but unless there's some
          clear, striking evidence for
          innocence and gross miscarriage
          of justice I will not interfere
          in the process.

He moves to collect his papers. Television lights are being
shut off. Some are beginning to rise and move from the table.

                    PREJEAN
          Governor.

He looks up at her.

                    PREJEAN
          I am Matt Poncelet's spiritual
          adviser. If he dies, I will be
          with him. Please don't let this
          man die.

Fredericks, a deft politician, immediately looks concerned.

                    FREDERICKS
          Can you do that? Can you watch
          that?

                    PREJEAN
          I promised him, Governor.

                    FREDERICKS
          I'll give the case careful
          consideration.

                    PREJEAN
          You can spare him. You have the
          power to prevent this death.

                    FREDERICKS
          I will look into the matter.

And he is gone. Amid the commotion:

                    HILTON
          Let's not give up on the
          courts. We still might hit pay
          dirt with one of the issues.

128   INT. PREJEAN'S MOTHER'S HOUSE. NIGHT.   128

Prejean lays in a bedroom. We hear sounds from the other
room. Her name is being called, once, twice. She is being
called to dinner. She gets up from the cot, walks down a
hallway, comes into a dining room with a round table. Her
mother is there as are her sister, brother, Sister Colleen,
Hilton Barber, and...Matt Poncelet. Matt is dressed in a
red and black plaid shirt and is smiling. Walter and Hope
are there. Prejean turns around and, at the end of the long
hallway she has just walked through we see the ten-year-old
Helen holding a stick, a possum at her feet.

129   INT. PREJEAN'S MOTHER'S HOUSE. NIGHT.   129

                  MOTHER
       Helen, you OK?

She touches her cheek, rubs her arm. A mother and her ten-
year-old girl. We are then CLOSE on Prejean, current time.

                  PREJEAN
       I was just dreaming, mama.

                  MOTHER
       What time do you have to be
       there?

                  PREJEAN
       Nine sharp.

                  MOTHER
       Did you set a clock?

                  PREJEAN
       Yes, mama.

A pause.

                  PREJEAN
       It's all so bizarre. A man is
       going to die in front of me
       tomorrow.

                  MOTHER
       Has he admitted to anything?

                  PREJEAN
       No, mama.

                        (CONTINUED)

129   CONTINUED: **129**

> MOTHER
> You're in deep water, kid.

> PREJEAN
> He's a tough one, doesn't give
> me much to love, lets me down,
> makes me angry, but I guess I
> believe that if I continue to
> show him love, give him respect
> that sooner or later he'll come
> around.

> MOTHER
> Do you remember when you gave
> me a black eye?

> PREJEAN
> I had a fever.

> MOTHER
> You were delirious, hysterical,
> screaming.

> PREJEAN
> I ran out of the house. What
> happened?

> MOTHER
> I had to tackle you, hold you
> so tight, you were trying to
> get up and run into the street.
> You socked me in the eye, you
> said you hated me, you
> screamed, but I held you. I
> held you tight. A mother's
> arms are strong when her
> child's in danger.

A130   EXT. PREJEAN'S MOTHER'S HOUSE. DAWN.   **A130**

Helen sits on the steps of the porch, unable to sleep.

130   INT. DEATH HOUSE. DAY.   **130**

    TITLE: EXECUTION DAY: 9:00 A.M.

                    MATT
          I didn't sleep last night. I
          wouldn't take that nerve
          medicine they tried to give me.
          I'm looking death in the eyes.
          I'm getting ready to go.

Matt looks down.

                  PREJEAN
          Listen, Matt, I want you to
          know that I respect your need
          for privacy. If you prefer to
          be alone or just with your
          family today I won't be
          offended.

                  MATT
          You should be here ma'am, if it
          won't put you out too much. I'm
          gonna want someone to talk to
          and be with right up to the
          end.

Matt shivers, starts.

                  MATT
          If only I knew I'd die right
          away when I get the first shot.
          Will I feel it? The lungs go
          first. Like a fast choke.
          That's gotta hurt. They say the
          body doesn't move, doesn't
          shake. My poor mama...

131   INT. BELIVEAU'S OFFICE. DAY.   **131**

Prejean on the phone. Matt is taking the polygraph test. We
do not hear the questions and answers or see the needle on
the machine.

                  PREJEAN
          Any word from the Fifth
          Circuit?

                               (CONTINUED)

> HILTON (V.O.)
> None yet. A good sign. They've
> had it a good while now and
> maybe that means they see
> something substantive in the
> petition. I gotta go.

> PREJEAN
> Alright, Hilton, I'll see you.

Beliveau sits at his desk.

> BELIVEAU
> Tell me something, Sister.
> What's a nun doing in a place
> like this? Shouldn't you be
> teaching children? Do you know
> what this man has done, the
> kids he killed?

> PREJEAN
> What he did was evil, I don't
> condone it. I just don't see
> much sense in doing the same to
> him. Killing people who kill
> people to show that killing is
> wrong...

> BELIVEAU
> You know how the Bible says
> "eye for an eye"...

> PREJEAN
> And you know that Jesus called
> us to go beyond that kind of
> vengeance, not to pay back an
> "eye for an eye," not to return
> hate for hate.

Beliveau holds up his hands.

> BELIVEAU
> I ain't gonna get into all this
> Bible quotin' with a nun, 'cuz
> I'm gonna lose.

They share a laugh.

(CONTINUED)

131   CONTINUED: (2)   131

                              PREJEAN
                    You know something, the Bible
                    also calls for death as
                    punishment for adultery,
                    prostitution, homosexuality,
                    profaning the Sabbath, trespass
                    upon sacred ground, and
                    contempt of parents.

                              BELIVEAU
                    Got me on two of those.

A132   EXT. DEATH HOUSE. HELEN'S POV. DAY.   A132

       We see the strap-down team in rehearsal.

132   INT. DEATH HOUSE. DAY.   132

       Matt's mother Lucille and her three sons, Matt's
       stepbrothers, MITCH, TROY, and JIM are sitting in folding
       metal chairs by the white metal door. Mitch and Troy sit
       closest to the door. Lucille and Jim sit behind. They are
       handsome, healthy-looking kids. Mitch, eighteen, the
       oldest, is the one keeping the conversation going.

                              MITCH
                    She was only on the phone a few
                    minutes and there she was
                    falling for the ole Matt charm.
                    I had to take back that phone.
                    Trying to steal my gal, you
                    dog.

       Matt laughs. Prejean pulls up a chair and looks at her
       watch. It's 4:10.

                              MATT
                    She sounds like a great little
                    lady.

                              JIM
                    She ain't so little.

                              MATT
                    You take care of her, Mickey.
                    Don't do nothing stupid.

                                                       (CONTINUED)

                              MITCH
            She looks a little like, what
            was that girlfriend you had in
            high school?

                              MATT
            I had a lot of girls in high
            school.

                              MITCH
            The one with the funny name.

                              MATT
            Funny name.

                              MITCH
            Maddie or Maldy or...

                              MATT
            Madrigal.

                              MITCH
            Madrigal Parmelee! That's it.
            She was hot.

                              MATT
            She was a nasty one, boy.

                              LUCILLE
            Matthew!

                              MATT
            Sorry, Mom. Madrigal was a fine
            upstanding young woman.

Mitch laughs.

                              MATT
            So what about you, Troy. You
            got a lil' girlfriend?

Troy is ten years old. His ears and the sides of his cheeks
and neck turn pink.

                                        (CONTINUED)

132 CONTINUED: (2)   132

                         TROY
               I don't have time for girls,
               too much fishing and camping to
               do.

                         LUCILLE
               Troy just got a new tent.

                         MATT
               What kind of tent you got?

                         TROY
               Army tent. I don't like those
               sissy tents with all them colors.

                         JIM
               Tell Matt about the other night
               in the backyard.

The others laugh.

                         MITCH
               Camping in the backyard.

                         LUCILLE
               I made him come in. I was
               worried. I went out there and
               made him come into the house.

Troy stands up near the door and moves his fingers up and
down the mesh screen.

                         TROY
               Me and my buddy Paul put up the
               tent and cooked our own dinner.
               We roasted these potatoes in
               tin foil on the fire and cooked
               us some weenies.

                         JIM
               Then what happened?

                         TROY
               Shut up.

                                            (CONTINUED)

132   CONTINUED: (3)   **132**

                              JIM
                Tell him.

                              TROY
                About midnight we hear some
                kind of animal walkin' around
                and making noises -- a strange
                animal. It was big and nasty.

Everyone laughs.

                              MATT
                Which is it? Did you come
                inside because of mama or
                because you was wigged out?

Mitch taps Troy on the shoulder.

                              MITCH
                Tell the truth now, tell the truth.

Troy is shifting from foot to foot. He finally smiles.
Everyone laughs. After the laugh a silence. A long
interminable silence.

                              LUCILLE
                Some people been asking me
                about your funeral. I get real
                angry and tell them "He's not
                dead."

Another silence.

133   EXT. DEATH HOUSE. DAY.   **133**

Prejean waits outside of the visiting room, taking a break,
looking overwhelmed. The guard, Trapp, approaches her.

                              TRAPP
                Sister, can I talk to you?

                              PREJEAN
                Sure thing, Sgt. Trapp.

                              TRAPP
                Not here.

134 EXT. DEATH HOUSE. DAY.[32]   **134**

Trapp walks with Prejean. He whispers. This is a troubled
man.

> TRAPP
>
> I've been through two of these
> executions and I can't eat, I
> can't sleep. I'm not sayin'
> these guys ain't bad. They done
> terrible crimes. They belong in
> here. This guy we killed,
> Roland Tobias. He shit himself
> when we came to get him. He
> cried like a baby. He said
> "Please don't. I'm sorry.
> I'm sorry." After he was dead I
> had to pack up his stuff to
> send to his family. He drawn
> this picture of heaven to send
> to his niece. "Me in heaven" it
> said, looked like a third
> grader's writin' with a little
> stick figure sitting on a
> cloud, waving.

A pause.

> TRAPP
>
> I can't get that out of my
> head, that little stick figure.
> Sister, I ain't got no problem
> with killin' nobody. I served
> my country proudly in Nam. I
> killed men before. But them
> guys had guns. Kill or be
> killed, you know? These here
> guys can't defend themself.
> We're draggin' 'em, holdin' 'em
> down. It ain't fair, makes you
> feel dirty.

> PREJEAN
>
> You've got to change your job.
> Can you do that?

(CONTINUED)

134 CONTINUED: **135**

> TRAPP
> I've put in for a transfer. But
> they gonna ask me questions. I
> try to be a good man but... I'm
> sorry to talk your ear off, I
> just can't really talk about
> this with people around here.

We HOLD on Helen.

135 INT. DEATH HOUSE. DUSK.   **135**

We are in the middle of an interminable silence.[33] Prejean
is back in the room, and everyone is talked out. From
Helen's POV we see Walter and Hope walking hand in hand by
the water. Suddenly, a CLANG and Warden Hartman appears at
the door.

> HARTMAN
> I'm sorry folks. We're going to
> have to wrap this up.

> MATT
> Already? Isn't it kind of
> early? Rules say they can stay
> until 6:45.

> HARTMAN
> It's time for you folks to be
> leaving now.

Matt stands up.

> MATT
> Listen, I put my stuff in two
> pillow-cases and I'd feel
> better if you guys took it home
> with you now. I don't want the
> prison sending it.

The GUARD on watch at the end of the tier moves to get the
white bags.

(CONTINUED)

135 CONTINUED: (2)   **135**

> GUARD
> Step back to the wall.

Matt does as he is told as the Guard opens the door. He
gathers the bag and hands them to Captain Beliveau.

> MATT
> Craig, ya'll can see about
> dividin' it up. Except my boots
> from Marion. I'm gonna walk to
> the execution in these here
> boots. No cryin' now. I don't
> want no cryin'. I'm not tellin'
> ya'll good-bye yet. I'll call
> you tonight.

> MITCH
> See ya, man. Stay strong.

There is a crack in his voice when he says "strong." Jim
and Troy are beginning to walk out. Troy's face is
beginning to crumble into tears. Mitch and Lucille are
moving toward the foyer. Lucille keeps jabbing a Kleenex to
her eyes.

> LUCILLE
> We love you, Mattie.

> MATT
> No cryin'. I'll call you
> tonight. I'll call you.

Lucille kisses Matt and turns and leaves.

136 INT. DEATH HOUSE - FRONT DOOR. DUSK.   **136**

Prejean puts her arm around Lucille and walks her to the
front door.

> LUCILLE
> If I had put my arms around my
> boy no guard could have got me
> to let go.

(CONTINUED)

136   CONTINUED: 137

She turns and goes through the door to the outside. Prejean
watches through the front glass door as the boys get into
the van. Lucille has thrown herself against a car and is
sobbing uncontrollably. Mitch stands awkwardly next to her.

                    MATT
          Is my mama doin OK?

                    PREJEAN
          Yes, Matt.

Meanwhile the guards are bringing in Matt's last meal.

137   INT. DEATH HOUSE. SUNSET.   137

Matt eats his food. She looks down at her food. It is
darkening outside.

                    MATT
          Never had shrimp before. They
          pretty good.

A pause.

                    MATT
          So what's the word on the lie
          detector test?

                    PREJEAN
          Culp said your answers showed
          stress, just as he had
          predicted. He said the results
          were inconclusive.

                    MATT
          Man! Is the dude sure? Is he
          absolutely, positively sure? I
          felt cool answering all them
          questions. I didn't feel no
          stress. Man! I can't believe I
          failed that test.

                                              (CONTINUED)

137 CONTINUED: 139

> PREJEAN
> Matt, you'd have to be a robot
> or insane not to feel stress
> now.

A pause.

> MATT
> Man! I just can't believe that
> test didn't come out right.

> PREJEAN
> Let's talk about what happened.
> Let's talk about that night.

> MATT
> I don't wanna talk about that.

138 EXT. LOUISIANA WOODS(1988). NIGHT - IMAGINED.   138

We see, facing the camera, the kneeling bodies of WALTER
DELACROIX and HOPE PERCY. They are terrified. Hope's shirt
is ripped, her breasts exposed. She is weeping. A gun
enters frame, pointed at the head of Walter. We whip PAN as
the shot is fired and are now TIGHT on Hope's face,
paralyzed with fear.

139 INT. DEATH HOUSE. NIGHT.[34]   139

Matt is in the middle of a tirade.

> MATT
> I'm pissed off. I'm pissed at
> those kids for being parked out
> in the woods. I'm pissed that
> their parents are coming to
> watch me die. I'm pissed at
> myself for letting Vitello get
> over them kids. But I got my
> last words coming. And I got a
> thing or two to say Percys and
> Delacroixs.

(CONTINUED)

> PREJEAN
> Do you want your last words to
> be words of hatred?

> MATT
> Clyde Percy's said he wants to
> inject me hisself!

> PREJEAN
> Well think about how angry he
> must be. He's never gonna see
> his daughter again. He's never
> gonna hug her. He's never
> gonna love her, laugh with her.
> You've robbed these parents of
> so much, Matt. They've got
> nothing in their lives but
> sorrow, no joy. That's what you
> have given them.

We are TIGHT on Prejean, disturbed.

> PREJEAN
> What possessed you to be in the
> woods that night?

> MATT
> I told ya, I was stoned outta my head.

> PREJEAN
> Now don't blame the drugs,
> Matt. You'd been harassing
> couples for weeks before this
> happened. Months! What was it?

> MATT
> What do you mean?

> PREJEAN
> What was it? Did you look up to
> Vitello? Did you think he was
> cool? Did you want to impress
> him?

(CONTINUED)

                         MATT
              I don't know.

                         PREJEAN
              You could have just walked
              away.

                         MATT
              He went psycho on me.

                         PREJEAN
              Stop blaming him. You blame
              him, you blame the government,
              you blame the drugs, you blame
              blacks. You blame the Percys.
              You blame the kids for being
              there. What about Matthew
              Poncelet? Where is he in this
              story? Just an innocent? Just a
              victim?

                         MATT
              I ain't no victim.

Matt gives her an intense, hard look. From Prejean's POV we
see the forms of two bodies, Walter Delacroix and Hope
Percy, sitting behind Matt. They are alive yet still,
emotionless, yet focused. The PHONE RINGS. Through the
door we see Captain Beliveau answer the phone. His
conversation is brief. He says something to Warden Hartman.
Hartman nods his head and walks out of the room. Beliveau
looks through the grate at Prejean and shakes his head, no.
Warden Hartman appears and says, matter-of-factly:

                         HARTMAN
              Poncelet, the Federal Appeals
              Court turned you down. I'm
              sorry.

TELEPHONE RINGS. Beliveau appears at the door

                         BELIVEAU
              Sister, please step into the
              corridor.

                                             (CONTINUED)

139 CONTINUED: (3)   **140**

>   PREJEAN
>   I'll be right outside.

Matt gets up and walks to the phone. Prejean looks down at
her food. Matt answers the phone, listens, then:

>   MATT
>   Thank you, Mr. Hilton, thank
>   you for what you and all the
>   others done for me. I got you
>   too late. If I had had you
>   sooner...(silence)...no, Mr.
>   Hilton, no you didn't fail. I
>   appreciate everything you and
>   the others have done for me. I
>   shoulda got you sooner. No,
>   you didn't fail. The justice
>   system in this country failed.
>   It stinks. It stinks bad.

She does so. A guard called SUMMERS comes through the front
door. He is big, burly, with a shiny bald head, and he is
carrying a small canvas bag. Summers, accompanied by TWO
OTHER GUARDS, goes into the cell with Matt.

140 INT. DEATH HOUSE FOYER. NIGHT.[35]   **140**

Prejean walks up and down foyer. Chaplain Farley approaches
her.

>   FARLEY
>   Sister, I will be administering
>   communion to Poncelet before he
>   makes his final walk.

>   PREJEAN
>   He has asked me to receive it
>   for both of us.

>   FARLEY
>   Well, that's unfortunate.

>   PREJEAN
>   Pardon?

(CONTINUED)

> FARLEY
> You have been unable to provide
> enough spiritual guidance to
> this man as is evidenced in the
> fact that he will leave this
> earth without receiving the
> sacred sacrament of communion.

> PREJEAN
> Chaplain Farley, how are you at
> peace with what you do?

> FARLEY
> Excuse me?

> PREJEAN
> You take a salary from an
> institution that takes human
> life. How can you reconcile
> that with the teachings of
> Jesus Christ?

> FARLEY
> I take a small salary to
> provide spiritual counsel to
> people who need it. I try to
> draw them closer to God in
> their final days. I do not
> encourage them, as I assume you
> do, to reject the authority
> that leads them to this fate.

Captain Beliveau approaches.

> BELIVEAU
> Sister, you can go back to the
> cell now.

> PREJEAN
> Father.

She turns and walks with Beliveau.

141   INT. DEATH HOUSE. NIGHT.   141

TITLE: 10:30 P.M.

Summers comes through door on tier. Matt comes back to the
metal chair. His left pant leg has been cut off at the
knee.

                    MATT
          They shaved the calf of my leg.

He holds out his leg for her to see. There is a tattooed
number.

                    PREJEAN
          Why?

                    MATT
          I guess they was worried they
          won't find a vein in my arm.

                    PREJEAN
          What's that number?

                    MATT
          That's when I was at Marion.
          In case anybody killed me, I
          wanted them to be able to
          identify my body.

He is wearing a clean white T-shirt. He is no longer
wearing his long-sleeved denim shirt. She sees for the
first time that his arms are covered in tattoos. He lowers
his eyes, not wanting to look at her, and says:

                    PREJEAN
          Did it hurt when you did all
          those?

                    MATT
          No. You're gonna think I'm a
          bad person, seeing all these
          tattoos.

                                        (CONTINUED)

141   CONTINUED: 141

He is very embarrassed. There is a swastika and a skull,
women's names, and on one arm a naked woman.

                    PREJEAN
          Nah, you just have more color
          on you than I thought.

Matt lights a cigarette. Everything is ready now. Inside
the tier, TWO GUARDS stand on stepladders and hang black
curtains over the windows along the top.

                    MATT
          They don't want anyone seeing
          in, I guess.

A pause.

                    MATT
          They tried to give me two
          shots. I wouldn't let em. Tried
          to give me a sedative and an
          antihistamine.

                    PREJEAN
          An antihistamine?

                    MATT
          Said in case I have an allergic
          reaction to the first shot that
          knocks me out. Could get messy.

A guard brings in a telephone and sets it next to Matt.

                    MATT
          Time to call home.

Prejean gets up to leave.

                    MATT
          Will you stay?

                    PREJEAN
          I'll stay, I'll just give you
          some privacy.

142   INT. DEATH HOUSE. NIGHT.   142

She stands by the door.

As Matt makes his phone call we intercut between Matt and
what Prejean sees outside the cell. The last-minute
preparations for the execution have begun. The building is
buzzing now. Guards are everywhere and men in three-piece
suits. A buffet has been set out with sandwiches. A
secretary has arrived and has begun typing. You can hear
the click, click, click of the typewriter. It sounds like a
business office. Prejean whispers to Beliveau.

>   PREJEAN
> What's she typing?

>   BELIVEAU
> Forms for the witnesses to
> sign.

143   INT. BATHROOM. NIGHT.   143

The cold, preordained cruelty of it all hits her. Prejean
puts both hands against the tiled wall, puts her head down
and prays.

>   PREJEAN
> Oh, Jesus. God help me. I'm so
> scared.

She trembles, falls to her knees.

>   PREJEAN
> This is a terrifying place,
> God. So cold, so calculated,
> this death. Just don't let him
> fall apart, God. Please help
> him. Help me, Jesus.

144 INT. DEATH HOUSE. NIGHT.   144

A large aluminum coffee pot is percolating fresh coffee. A
white tablecloth has been put on a table and ball-point
pens have been placed in the center of the table. Matt is
crying, sobbing. He hangs up the phone. He blows his nose
and quickly regains his composure.

                    MATT
          I just let it flow. I told my
          mama that I loved her. I talked
          to each of the boys. I hated to
          say good-bye. I told them that
          if I get a chance I'll call 'em
          back right before I go.

There is a pause. Matt breaks down. He begins to sob.

                    PREJEAN
          What is it Matt?

                    MATT
          My mother said, "It was that
          Vitello. I'll always regret
          that you got involved with
          him." And I didn't want her to
          think that. Something you said.
          I could have walked away. But I
          didn't. I let myself listen to
          him. I was a victim, a fuckin'
          chicken. He was older, tough as
          hell. I was all boozed up
          trying to be as tough as him. I
          didn't have the guts to stand up
          to him. I told my mother I was
          yellow, goin' along with him. I
          didn't stand up to him. My mother
          kept saying, "No, Matt, it wasn't
          you, it wasn't you."

He sobs. Long beat.

                    PREJEAN
          Your mama loves you, Matt.

                    MATT
          That boy, Walter...

                                        (CONTINUED)

144   CONTINUED: 144

                         PREJEAN
            Yeah, What Matt?

                         MATT
            I killed him.

                         PREJEAN
            And Hope?

                         MATT
            No ma'am.

                         PREJEAN
            Did you rape her?

                         MATT
            Yes ma'am.

                         PREJEAN
            Do you take responsibility for
            both of their deaths?

                         MATT
            Yes ma'am.

A pause.

                         MATT
            Last night when they dimmed the
            lights on the tier I kneeled
            down by my bunk and prayed for
            them kids. I never done that
            before.

The silence is heavy. Prejean stands up and puts her hands
against the metal screen door, getting as close to him as
possible.

                         PREJEAN
            Oh, Matt, there are spaces of
            sorrow that only God can touch.
            You did a terrible thing, Matt,
            a terrible thing. But you have
            a dignity now and no one can
            take that from you. You are a
            son of God, Matthew Poncelet.

                                          (CONTINUED)

144   CONTINUED: (2)   144

                              MATT
                    Ain't nobody never called me no
                    son of God before. (smiling)
                    I've been called a son-of-a-
                    you-know-what lots of times but
                    never no son of God. I just
                    hope my death gives their
                    parents some relief. I really
                    do.

                              PREJEAN
                    Maybe that's the best thing you
                    can offer the Delacroixs and the
                    Percys, a wish for their peace.

A pause.

                              MATT
                    You know, I've never known real
                    love, never loved women or
                    anybody all that well myself.
                    Figures I'd have to go to my
                    death to find love.

He looks directly at Prejean.

                              MATT
                    Thank you for loving me.

They can hear the front door opening and closing over and
over. The witnesses and press are arriving.

                              MATT
                    Getting busy around here.

Prejean looks at the clock: 11:30.

                              MATT
                    Look at the time, it's flying.

Prejean is terrified. She puts her trembling fingers to her
mouth and grabs hold of the crucifix around her neck.
Matt's moment of weakness passed, he sits in metal chair
and calls to Beliveau for a cup of coffee. He pulls a
cigarette from the pack in his shirt pocket and notices
that there are just a few left:

                                                   (CONTINUED)

144   CONTINUED: (3)   **144**

                              MATT
                  Ought to just about make it.

He shivers.

                              MATT
                  It's cold in here.

                              PREJEAN
                  Can somebody get him a shirt.
                  He's cold.

The guard gets a blue denim shirt and puts it around Matt's
shoulders.

                              MATT
                  What happened to that song you
                  were going to play me?

                              PREJEAN
                  The hymn.

                              MATT
                  Yeah, that.

                              PREJEAN
                  They have rules forbidding
                  music in the prison.

                              MATT
                  Yeah.

                              PREJEAN
                  They won't let me play it.

                              MATT
                  You can sing it. You know the
                  words?

                              PREJEAN
                  I can't sing.

                                              (CONTINUED)

144 CONTINUED (4)   **144**

>   MATT
>   That's okay. Come on.

There is a pause and then, Prejean begins singing "Be Not Afraid" softly at first. Matt listens, at first amused and then gradually more and more moved.

>   PREJEAN
>   If you cross the barren desert
>   you shall not die of thirst
>   be not afraid,
>   I go before you always
>   if you stand before
>   the fires of hell
>   and death is at your side
>   be not afraid

As she finishes Matt has a tear in his eye.

>   MATT
>   Thank you.

A team of GUARDS comes into the cell. They take him to a bathroom and shut the door behind him. She hears the murmur of voices. She hears the toilet flush. Beliveau stands near Prejean.

The bathroom door opens and the guards and Matt reenter the room. Anger flickers in Matt's eyes.

>   MATT
>   Give me back my boots. I want
>   my boots. A grown man, and I
>   have to leave this world with a
>   diaper on, walking in slippers.

He shakes his handcuffs defiantly.

>   MATT
>   I'll be free from all this. No
>   more cells, no more bars, no
>   more life in a cage.

145   INT. DEATH HOUSE. NIGHT.   **145**

TITLE: 11:45 P.M.

Prejean stands outside the cell. The GUARDS inside are
putting the shackles on Matt's hands and feet inside cell.
Warden Hartman approaches them, flanked by six or seven
large guards, including Trapp; the "Strap-Down Team."

>   HARTMAN
>   Time to go, Poncelet.

A GUARD opens the cell door and Matt comes over to the
metal folding chair by the door. As he approaches the chair
his legs sag and he drops to one knee beside the chair. He
looks up at Prejean:

>   MATT
>   Sister Helen, I'm going to die.

>   PREJEAN
>   But you know the truth now,
>   Matt, and the truth has set
>   you free.

>   MATT
>   God knows the truth about me.
>   I'm going to a better place.
>   I'm not worried at all.

But he is shivering and the Guard comes and puts his denim
jacket around his shoulders. People are chatting nervously
in the foyer. The witnesses are inside, the press, prison
officials. You can hear the hum of talk and the sound of
coins being inserted into the drink machines and the clunk
of cans. We see Earl Delacroix and the Percys.

>   MATT
>   Are you OK?

>   (CONTINUED)

145 CONTINUED: **145**

>   PREJEAN
> Yeah, Matt. I'm OK. Christ is
> here. Look, I want the last
> thing you see in this world to
> be a face of love. Look at me.
> When they do this, look at me.
> I will be the face of Christ
> for you.

>   MATT
> Yes ma'am.

>   HARTMAN
> Let's go.

Helen puts her hand on his shoulder. They walk. The chains
scrape across the floor. A guard shouts:

>   BELIVEAU
> Dead Man Walkin'!

Prejean, carrying her Bible, reads from Isaiah 43:2. As she
reads the words she looks up and sees that Matt is walking
with the same little jaunty walk, up on the balls of his
feet.

>   PREJEAN
> Do not be afraid I have called
> you by your name, you are mine.
> Should you pass through the
> sea, I will be with you. Should
> you walk through the fire, you
> will not be scorched, and the
> flames will not burn you.

146 INT. DEATH HOUSE LOBBY. NIGHT.   **146**

As they pass through the lobby Chaplain Farley raises
his hand in blessing. They stop.

>   (CONTINUED)

146   CONTINUED: 147

                         BELIVEAU
          That's as far as you go sister.

                         MATT
          Sister will you look in on my
          mama from time to time?

                         PREJEAN
          You have my word on that.

Prejean leans toward Matt and kisses him on the back. The
guards guide Prejean away into the execution room to a
chair with the other witnesses.

147   INT. EXECUTION ROOM. NIGHT.   147

There is a gurney, gleaming in the bright fluorescent
lights. There are the witnesses all seated behind a
Plexiglas window. There is a big clock on the wall behind
the chair. Hilton Barber is there. Prejean sits in a chair
beside Hilton. He reaches over and takes her hand. Hilton
does not look into her eyes. Mr. Delacroix and the Percys
are seated in the first row over to the right, their faces
expressionless. There is a small podium with a microphone
on it, and Matt is standing behind it. The Warden is
standing over in the right-hand corner next to the
telephone.

                         HARTMAN
          Have any last words, Poncelet?

                         MATT
          Yes, sir, I do.

He looks at the two fathers, but then addresses himself
only to Delacroix:

                                             (CONTINUED)

147 CONTINUED: 148

> MATT
> Mr. Delacroix, I don't want to
> leave this world with any
> hatred in my heart. I want to
> ask your forgiveness for what I
> did. I have done a terrible
> thing in taking your son from
> you.

Delacroix nods his head. Clyde turns to Delacroix and asks:

> CLYDE
> What about us?

> MATT
> I would just like to say, Mr.
> and Mrs. Percy, that I hope you
> get some relief from my death.

Matt on the gurney now and the guards are moving quickly,
removing the leg irons and handcuffs and replacing them
with leather straps. One guard removes his left slipper.
They strap his trunk, his legs, his arms. Matt finds
Prejean's face. A nurse swabs his arm with alcohol, then
puts an IV needle in.

> MATT
> I love you.

She stretches her hand toward him.

> PREJEAN
> I love you, too.

He attempts a smile but manages only a twitch. The IV leads
from Matt's arm to the lethal injection machine.

> HILTON
> Father forgive them.

Only the Warden, Beliveau, and Summers remain in the room
now. Warden nods his head. Beliveau and Summers both push a
button on the lethal injection machine.

THREE CLICKS are heard.

148   EXT. PRISON PARKING LOT. NIGHT.[36]   148

There are lights blazing everywhere and a TACTICAL TEAM
lined up along the front fence. Prejean is with Colleen
and the other nuns from her order. They all hug and kiss
and cry. Prejean turns to see Earl Delacroix. He looks
shaken and the rims of his eyes are red. He walks past.

149   EXT. PRISON PARKING LOT. NIGHT.   149

We see Clyde Percy, cameras all around him as he pops a
bottle of champagne and pours himself a drink. He smiles.

                         CLYDE
               I'm just sorry every victim
               doesn't have the satisfaction
               of watching a murderer die. But
               you know what? He died too
               quick, too easy. I wish he had
               the same kind of painful death
               that my daughter had. I hope he
               fries in hell for all eternity.

                         REPORTER
               Are you happy, Mr. Percy?

                         CLYDE
               Do you want to dance?

                         REPORTER
               How about you, Mrs. Percy?

                         MARYBETH
               I'm glad he's dead and won't be
               able to kill any other people.

Emily is there and pipes in:

                         EMILY
               This is the best I've felt in a
               long time, knowing the man who
               killed my sister has finally
               been executed. That ought to
               tell murderers that if they
               kill somebody, they're going to
               get killed themselves.

150   EXT. PARKING LOT. NIGHT.   150

Prejean and the Sisters head to the car waiting in the
parking lot. Hilton walks with them.

> HILTON
> There was a time in this
> country when over 70 percent of
> the people favored slavery.
> You've got to keep at this.
> This is a long fight. Sooner or
> later people will come around.

> PREJEAN
> Thank you, Hilton.

They hug.

> HILTON
> I'll see you tomorrow.

Helen turns and sees her Mother, getting out of her car.

> MOTHER
> Hey, kid.

> PREJEAN
> Hi, mama.

They hug.

> MOTHER
> You know, it's not so much
> about success. It's the effort.
> You do what you do because you
> believe it's right. When we
> try, God is there.

151   OMITTED   151

152   INT. FUNERAL HOME - SLIDELL, LA. DAY.   152

A handful of friends and relatives have gathered to bury
Matt. We see Lucille and her sons, Prejean, Hilton, others.
Matt's brothers hover close to their mother. Little Troy
keeps taking her hand and holding it. Prejean is there.
Mitch reads a letter from Matt.

(CONTINUED)

152 CONTINUED: **152**

> MITCH
>
> "Dear my brothers, Don't worry
> about me, I'll be okay. You
> keep your cool, it's the only
> way to stay out of places like
> this. I been pretty stupid and
> I've done some bad things.
> When you think of me, remember
> times I made you laugh, times
> we wrestled, fun times. You can
> remember this bad boy, this
> rebel, if you want, but don't
> think that's cool. I was a
> coward, and I killed a man.
> Ain't nothin' cool about that.

As the letter continues we see a small procession of people
file past the coffin of Matthew Poncelet.

> MATT (V.O.)
>
> "Take care of mama. Remember
> the promise you made to me. I
> love you all. Your big brother.
> And P.S. to Troy: It's all
> right to be afraid. Sometimes
> there really are big animals
> outside your tent."

Lucille approaches the casket. She is weeping.

> LUCILLE
>
> Oh, Mattie, Mattie, my boy, Oh
> God, help me. Oh, Mattie, how
> much I loved you.

As she weeps we see for a moment MaryBeth Percy in her
place. Lucille then bends down and kisses the cold, still
lips of Walter Delacroix.

153 EXT. CEMETERY. DAY.   **153**

Bishop Todd says a short prayer. Over this we hear Matt's
voice. We see Prejean.

(CONTINUED)

153 CONTINUED: 153

                              MATT (V.O.)
                    Don't get all sad and mourn me,
                    OK? Do me a favor, will ya?
                    Maybe now and then go and pour
                    a beer on my grave.

Earl Delacroix appears in the distance. He stands still.
The service ends. The family is hugging, consoling each
other. Prejean walks to Delacroix.

                              PREJEAN
                    Mr. Delacroix.

                              DELACROIX
                    Sister.

                              PREJEAN
                    Thank you for coming.

                              DELACROIX
                    I don't know why I'm here. I
                    should go.

                              PREJEAN
                    Maybe you're looking for a way
                    out.

                              DELACROIX
                    It's a struggle. I've got a lot
                    of hate. I don't have your
                    faith.

                              PREJEAN
                    It's not faith. It's work.
                    Constant work.

There is a restless pause.

                              PREJEAN
                    Maybe we can try and find some
                    answers; the two of us.

                              DELACROIX
                    I don't know. I don't think so.

Delacroix leaves.

A154   INT. HOPE HOUSE. DAY.   A154

About twelve African American women sit around a table.
Helen is there. A woman speaks, her head down.

                         WOMAN
              I keep wanting to stay in bed
              and sleep and not get up. If I
              can just get through my boy's
              birthday, then Christmas...I've
              lost three children: the first
              was a crib death, my three-
              year-old dies of hepatitis, and
              now my twenty-four-year-old son
              was shot dead.

We hear the THREE CLICKS we heard when we cut away from the
execution.

154   INT. EXECUTION ROOM. NIGHT.   154

We are very CLOSE in on a clear liquid moving through a
tube. We come upon Matt's left hand which has gripped the
arm of the gurney. We see Matt's face, terrified.

155   EXT. LOUISIANA WOODS (1988). NIGHT - FLASHBACK.   155

Poncelet and Vitello creep along behind trees, bushes,
moving silently.

                         MATT
              I'll flush him out.

Matt throws a rock at a bush. Nothing.

                         MATT
              Little fucker split. Here
              bunny, here bunny.

                         VITELLO
              Matt, lookee here.

We see what Vitello sees. A car parked. A romantic tryst.

156   INT. EXECUTION ROOM. NIGHT.   156

We see the hand move slightly. We hear a soft moan
and...another Click.

The second liquid comes through the tube.

> WOMAN (V.O.)
> I keep waitin' for my boy to
> knock on the door. Seven times,
> that was his little knock and
> I'd say, "Who's there?" and
> he'd say, "Me, Baby," and the
> newspaper told it wrong. They
> talked about my boy's murder
> like it was just another drug-
> related murder. They don't know
> who shot my boy. The killer's
> still out there somewhere.

157   EXT. LOUISIANA WOODS (1988). NIGHT - FLASHBACK.   157

Poncelet and Vitello approach the parked car on either
side. The lovers continue their necking within. CLOSE on a
rifle butt hitting glass. Pull out to see the couple,
Walter Delacroix and Hope Percy, startled out of their
embrace, instantly terrified.

> MATT
> Excuse me, what are you doing?

> WALTER
> Oh, my God.

Vitello laughs.

> MATT
> This is private property. Y'all
> are trespassing.

> WALTER
> We didn't know.

> MATT
> Get out of the car.

157   CONTINUED: 157

    Vitello opens the door, pointing the gun at them, laughing.
    Matt puts handcuffs on the couple as they get out of the
    car.

158   INT. EXECUTION ROOM. NIGHT.   158

    The body relaxes. Then, suddenly, a quick spasm. A choked
    painful gasp. The eyes close in pain then relax, still
    closed. We hear a Click and....

                    WOMAN (V.O.)
            How do I introduce myself -- as
            the mother of six or the mother
            of four? I guess I'll say six
            even though two of my sons were
            killed, both of them shot, five
            months apart. I've been angry
            at God and confused because I
            have really tried to do right,
            go to church every Sunday, and
            give a good home to my kids and
            I thought that would protect
            us.

159   EXT. LOUISIANA WOODS (1988). NIGHT - FLASHBACK.   159

    Hope Percy is being raped by Matt Poncelet. She weeps
    inconsolably. Walter Delacroix is held by Vitello in the
    background.

                    WALTER
            Put down that gun and fight me
            like a man you chickenshit
            asshole.

                    MATT
            Kneel down.

                    HOPE
            Please, no.

                              (CONTINUED)

159 CONTINUED: 159

                         MATT
             If you don't do what we say,
             we're gonna shoot you. So kneel
             down.

                         WALTER
             Put down your gun. I'll take
             you both on.

                         VITELLO
             Oooh, he's a hero.

                         MATT
             If you don't kneel down we're
             gonna shoot you.

                         HOPE
             Walter, kneel down, please,
             kneel down. Do it now! I don't
             want to die.

After a moment Walter complies, joining his girlfriend,
knees in the Louisiana mud. A beat. Then: Gunshots.

160 INT. EXECUTION ROOM. NIGHT.   160

The body is basically still, a slight reflex in the leg,
then the eyes open. Matt is dead. Hartman motions to the
doctor to approach the body. The doctor, who has been
sitting with the witnesses, goes to the body in the gurney
and puts his hand over Matt's eyes, closing them. The
doctor puts his stethoscope against the heart, listens;
then turns to the Warden and nods his head. Chaplain
Farley's eyes happen to look into Prejean's. He lowers his
eyes. We see Sgt. Trapp.

161 INT. HOPE HOUSE. DAY.   161

Prejean and the Sisters run a victim's meeting with
neighborhood residents, mostly black. An African-American
woman addresses the others.

                                              (CONTINUED)

161   CONTINUED: 161

                              WOMAN
                I lost two sons in the St.
                Thomas Project. Both murdered,
                but the D.A. hasn't come close
                to prosecuting the case. They
                don't care much when black boys
                get killed. Everyday I see the
                boys that killed my sons.
                Everyday. And they know I know.
                And they laugh and leer.

Angle on Prejean, her expression grim but focused.

162   EXT. PERCY HOUSE BACKYARD. DAY.   162

Prejean and Clyde and Marybeth sit in the backyard. They
have drinks.

                              CLYDE
                I almost died in Vietnam. My
                ship was torpedoed. I was
                fished out of the sea
                unconscious, they thought I was
                dead, almost dumped me into a
                body bag. Then someone noticed
                that I was breathing. "Hey
                lookee here...."

We can tell that Clyde has told this story before in better
times. He can't seem to do it now. He starts to cry.

                              CLYDE
                I'm sorry. I just can't get
                over her death. I still want to
                see him suffer.

He tries to make a fist and strikes out but the air flows
through his fingers.

                              CLYDE
                What we really oughta do...
                ...we oughta do to them exactly
                what they did to their victim.
                              (MORE)

                                                          (CONTINUED)

162 CONTINUED: **162**

> CLYDE (CONT'D)
> Poncelet should be stabbed
> seventeen times then shot in
> the back of the head, that's
> what we oughta do to him.

We see Prejean. She puts her arm around Clyde, hugs him as
he weeps. We see Marybeth.

163 INT. PREJEAN APARTMENT. NIGHT.   **163**

INSERT: Dead Man Walking: An Eyewitness Account. Prejean
types as we hear:

> PREJEAN (V.O.)
> A million times I come back to
> his face, wild and torn,
> without reason or compassion or
> any of the calming signs we
> seek day to day in our
> companions. A million times I
> come back to his face, and this
> time, in this dream, his face
> is unrepentant, his eyes
> violent and dead, his hand
> holding a bloody knife. I hear
> the moaning of a dying person.
> Matt has just attacked someone
> I know, someone I love. The
> fireplace of my childhood home
> is stained with blood and in my
> hand I hold a weapon, and I
> raise the weapon up to him.
> Mahatma Ghandi once said, "If
> we were all to take an eye for
> an eye, the world would be
> blind." Jesus Christ showed us
> that the only way to stop the
> mad circle of violence and
> retribution was through love
> and justice.

Helen has stopped typing and moves to the window. A
flashing light hits her face.

164   EXT. ST. THOMAS PROJECT. NIGHT.   164

From Helen's POV. We see Herbie, the boy who was shot, in
handcuffs being put into a police car.

165   EXT. OUR LADY OF MERCY CHURCH - SLIDELL. DAWN.   165

Prejean walks in the early morning mist along a wooded
path. A hymn plays, redemptive, uplifting. We see a small
chapel come into view.

> PREJEAN (V.O.)
> ...Love for everyone, even
> those that inflict pain. For
> the family of a victim this
> is an emotion that seems
> unattainable, impossible.
> But perhaps there is redemption
> in reconciliation. Perhaps
> there is some peace in not
> letting the hatred overtake
> you. In not letting those that
> have hurt you continue to after
> they're gone. If we forgive, do
> our memories of our loved ones
> fade or do they become more
> pure? Only time will tell.

Prejean walks up the steps and lightly taps on the door of
the chapel and a young woman with long dark hair lets her
in with a quiet smile.

166   INT. OUR LADY OF MERCY CHURCH. DAWN.   166

Inside the chapel she sees a sign hand-printed in black
letters on white paper, a quotation from the Gospel of
John: "Because you have seen me, you believe. Blessed are
those who do not see and yet believe." The round wafer of
bread consecrated at Mass is elevated in a gold vessel with
clear glass at the center so the host can be seen. Gold
rays, emanating outward, draw the eye to the center.
Prejean sits in a pew. Behind her the doors open and in
walks Earl Delacroix. He approaches slowly and sits next to
Helen.

166 CONTINUED:

> DELACROIX
> You made it. I'm glad you're
> safe, you know these highways.

> PREJEAN
> It's good to see you, Mr.
> Delacroix.

> DELACROIX
> Earl.

Prejean smiles.

> PREJEAN
> Shall we get to work?

> DELACROIX
> Yes. Yes ma'am, let's do that.

They both kneel and begin to pray. The hymn ends. Silence.

STILLS

Above: Tim Robbins and Roger Deakins, the director of photography, gauge the next shot.

SISTER HELEN PREJEAN
Susan Sarandon

MATTHEW PONCELET
Sean Penn

Opposite: Sister Helen (*Susan Sarandon*) listens to Matthew Poncelet (*Sean Penn*), hours before his execution.

Above: Sister Helen Prejean (*Sarandon*) and Sister Colleen (*Margo Martindale*) participate in a vigil during a protest outside of Angola prison in the hours preceding an execution.

Below: Earl Delacroix (*Ray Barry*), the father of murder victim Walter Delacroix, prays with Sister Helen (*Sarandon*).

Above: Sister Helen (*Sarandon*) and Lucille Poncelet (*Roberta Maxwell*) look at photos of
  Matthew as a child during his pardon board hearing.
Below: Matthew Poncelet (*Penn*), Sister Helen (*Sarandon*), and Sister Colleen (*Martindale*)
  listen to testimony at Matthew's pardon board hearing.
Opposite: Sister Helen Prejean (*Sarandon*) visits with children from the community where
  she lives, at the St. Thomas Projects in New Orleans.

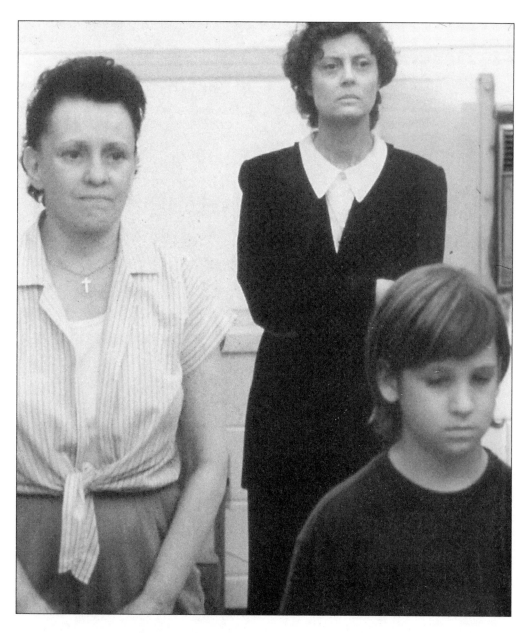

Opposite above: Sister Helen (*Sarandon*) and Matthew (*Penn*) consider their differences.

Opposite below: Matthew's family (*Roberta Maxwell, Jack Black, Jon Abrahams,* and *Arthur Bridgers*) just outside the death house moments after their final visit.

Above: Sister Helen (*Sarandon*) watches as Matthew's mother, Lucille Poncelet (*Maxwell*), and youngest brother, Troy *(Arthur Bridgers)*, prepare to leave after their final visit with Matthew on death row.

Above: Acting as his spiritual adviser, Sister Helen (*Sarandon*) listens to Matthew (*Penn*) after he has been moved to the death house in the final week before his execution.

Below: Sister Helen (*Sarandon*) reads to Matthew (*Penn*) from the Bible as they walk to the execution chamber together.

Above: Parents of both murder victims, Mary Beth Percy (*Celia Weston*), Clyde Percy (*R. Lee Ermey*), and Earl Delacroix (*Ray Barry*), sit in attendance at Matthew's execution.

Below: Sister Helen (*Sarandon*) reaches out to Matthew as the lethal injection process begins. Hilton Barber (*Robert Prosky*), Matthew's lawyer, sits to her left.

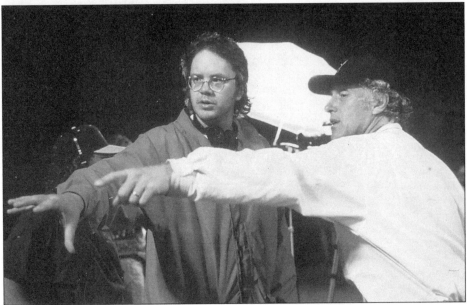

Above: Tim Robbins and Susan Sarandon enjoy a lighthearted moment between takes.
Below: Tim Robbins and Roger Deakins discuss the logistics of a shot outside the gate of
   Angola prison.
Opposite: Tim Robbins directs the actors involved in the protest outside the prison gates.

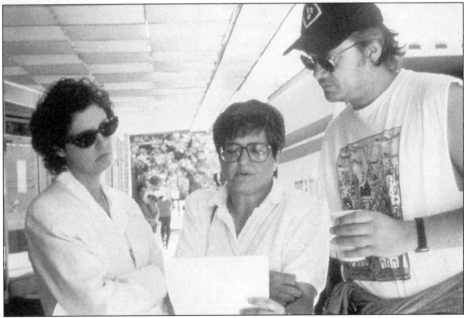

Above: Susan Sarandon and Tim Robbins discuss the next shot outside Lucille Poncelet's home.
Below: Susan Sarandon and Tim Robbins consult with Sister Helen Prejean.

Above: Sister Helen Prejean in a moment of contemplation while visiting the set.
Below: Susan Sarandon, Sister Helen Prejean, and Sam Cohn relax between takes.

Above: Susan Sarandon rehearses a scene in the death house as director Tim Robbins and other crew members look on.

Below: Sister Helen Prejean and Tim Robbins on the set in the death house.

Opposite: Susan Sarandon and Sean Penn discuss an upcoming scene in the death house.

Matthew Poncelet (*Sean Penn*) in his cell on the night of his impending execution.

SCENE NOTES

BY TIM ROBBINS

1. Scene 11. On the day of shooting we incorporated lines from this scene into the first scene in Hope House (scene 10). It created more motion and energy in scene 10 and allowed us to jump right to scene 13 without lines in scene 11 telling us what we will soon see in scene 13.

2. Scene 18. We shot this scene, but it did not wind up in the film. There were two problems. One was the rhythm of the scene was off. The child I had given most of the words to was distracted for some reason, and being faced with a daunting amount of work that day we had to move on without getting it properly. Children, I've learned, are on their own schedule on movie sets, and if there is a problem, the solution lies in relaxing and taking the time needed. The second, more important reason it isn't in the film is that the scene does not progress the story. When we saw the assembled footage it was readily apparent that we had to get right to the first visit between Prejean and Matthew. Anything else, regardless of how good the performances, slowed the story down.

3. Scenes 19–20. We shot these scenes intending to create a feeling of the neighborhood Sister Helen lived in. The scene had energy and a good performance by a local kid named Buck Horton but again had to be lost because we needed to get to the prison, to the first meeting.

4. Scene 36. We cut this line on the day of shooting. Lines like these tell an audience too much. They're helpful to an actor but really are more stage directions than lines. When you have an actor the caliber of Susan Sarandon it is much more interesting to view this emotion in silence, letting her eyes tell the story.

5. *Scene B39.* I liked this very much. Sean's performance was great. The speech ultimately became a tangent, a story that took us out of the moment, that reduced the tension of the first meeting. We did leave in the point of the story, that his daughter is in Texas somewhere, that he has lost touch with her; another child without a father.

6. *Scene 46.* In cutting this scene we found it wasn't interesting in a linear fashion. It became much more dreamlike when it was nonlinear.

7. *Scene 48.* a) Important information, but it stuck out. Too specific for the question asked.

b) Susan had a problem with this while we were shooting but gamely went ahead and tried it. She had good reason to have doubts. The writing is too aware for the moment and is better subtext than text. Prejean can't quite articulate her doubts or her compassion for the victims' families at this point. She does know that the visit with Poncelet made her uncomfortable, and by ending the scene where we did we end with doubt rather that articulated concern for the victims' families.

8. *Scene 49.* Scene 49 was cut because it is essentially about the subplot of Herbie's shooting, which we lost throughout the movie.

9. *Scene 50.* Scene 50 was lost because it slowed the momentum of the storytelling. By going right to scene 51 we are continuing the doubt and concern at the end of scene 48. We are also immediately looking into the files that Prejean takes at the end of scene 48.

10. *Scenes 52–54.* I had the four news reporters say all of the lines and then in editing crosscut and cross-mixed their reports so that a cacophonous feeling prevailed. We also used white noise, channel static, to help with the cuts. Quick storytelling, TV style.

11. *Scene 58.* a) Early in the shooting we covered a Governor Benedict "tough on crime speech." It was bothering me that Matthew's appearance on the television simultaneously with the phone call was unbelievable. On the day of the shooting we played Governor Benedict's speech under the phone call and placed the news report of Matthew's impending execution after the governor's speech.

b) Susan's contribution. "They're gonna kill me" is more direct and frankly more honest. Death-row inmates would not be vague about this.

12. Scene 61. A very difficult day of shooting. It was hot and humid, and the actors were stuck in a car. Car scenes are very difficult to do. On that day we rewrote and reconfigured this scene. The opening speech was later put in the pardon board scene. The scene as we shot it is different from what is here. Robert Prosky, who had arrived the night before, was a true professional and rolled with the frustrations of that day and the limitations of the scene as written.

13. Scene 64. Cut from movie. Despite fine performances by Robert and Susan it was one of those scenes that is talking about what we will soon see, sometimes necessary for a breather but oftentimes unnecessary. Pace determines everything at a certain point, and scenes like these are the first to go.

14. Scene A68. There were many people who thought this scene should be cut. I thought it was necessary to see Sister Helen's place of worship; the music was up-tempo and lifted the spirit of the moment, and most important my son Miles is in the scene.

15. Scene 69. A difficult cut to make. I liked the performances a lot, but it was just time to progress to the next scene. A curious thing I find in the cutting of a film is that you become a slave to pace and storytelling. As much as you love particular moments or performance nuances you find yourself serving this juggernaut of the story moving forward. It becomes your primary function, your responsibility.

16. Scene 70. This line came from Susan. I forget what earlier drafts had at this point but they were nowhere near this. This is the insight of an astute actor who is, in this line, inviting the audience into her experience, through simplicity and encompassing an ambiguity that neither Sister Helen nor I could put our finger on. When Sister Helen heard the line she exclaimed, "Yes, that's exactly how I felt."

17. Scene 71–73. Cut: not necessary; one beat too many away from Helen and Matt.

18. Scene 75. A spectacular performance by Robert Prosky but one too many beats in the speech. Had to lose this but hated to.

19. Scene B78. For me the depth of emotion, the sorrow and irony on Prosky's face on the line "Justice has been done" spoke volumes. What he achieved in that moment far outweighed the direct appeal to follow. We let it sit with the subtlety and the irony rather than overstate the obvious.

20. Scene 80. On the day of shooting this was incorporated into the earlier scene with Delacroix and Prejean. It gave us a cleaner out in this scene with "It's gonna be a tough road."

21. Scene 82. Subplot lost.

22. Scene 83. Totally unnecessary. We didn't even shoot it.

23. Scene 89. Cut from the movie. Did not progress story.

24. Scene 93. Took other nuns out of this scene. Without them we get more of a chance to know Colleen, and most important there was no way I was going to do a car scene with five people crammed into a hot space for six hours.

25. Scene 104. Susan, doing yet another scene where she is apologizing, joked one day that we should make a talking Sister Helen doll who, when you pull her string says, "I'm sorry," and, "I'm so sorry."

26. Scene A110. On the day of shooting we decided to get right to the point and started this line with "My wife filed for divorce today." The rest of the line has really already been said by other people in the room in one way or another. The design of the shot was always centered around a slow move in on Delacroix and a cacophony of voices that tell the story of the victims' families' pain and frustration.

27. Scene 114. On the day of shooting we added an abrupt interruption at this point. Without warning, the guards come in and take him away. We all thought it was important to do this. There is an oppressiveness to it; it's part of the constant mind game that happens in prison. The prisoner is always on guard, never really sure when things will happen, never prepared for anything. The guards can do what they want when they want. A prisoner doesn't have the power to say no or to even question. If one resists he will run into trouble, and it's only a matter of time before a prisoner relinquishes the misguided fallacy that he has any choice or any say or any self-determination.

28. *Scene A119.* A tough day. We got to this scene late in the day, people were tired, and we were trying to make up time lost to a flood that had covered New Orleans; all of the elements were against us. Not our finest hour, we tried to rework this scene, but it didn't work.

29. *Scene 122.* A good scene, well acted but nonessential to the drive of the story. We needed to get back to the Matt-Helen story, and there is no information or action in this scene that is crucial to the plot. It also suffered from the writing problem of placing an obstacle and removing the obstacle in the same scene. If something is going to be a threat, if it is possible that the warden is going to forbid further visits, then that must be true and allowed to sit at the end of the scene. Prejean must then, in subsequent scenes, regain her right to visit him. This is what happened in real life with Sister Helen. But the condensation of time would not allow for this tangent to be taken at this point. We didn't have the time to have her battle the warden and win. There was a much more important battle to be fought. We had to get back to Matt.

30. *Scene 124.* Shot the first part of this scene outside at dusk. Needed to open up a bit from confines of death row. Then we hard-cut to the interior where the press conference is.

31. *Scene 125.* This scene had to be cut substantially. By now the pace and momentum were clearly centered on Helen and Matt, and one could not stray from them for long.

32. *Scene 134.* This scene I hated to lose. It drove me nuts in the editing. The performances were incredibly strong, it was moving, it was an angle we haven't seen: the guard who is tortured by his involvement in the execution process. The problem was that as strong as it was, Matt and Helen had all the momentum. Matt was going to die that evening, and all we cared about was the two of them. Was she going to get through to him? Was he going to take responsibility? In a way, Trapp was too interesting. The power of the scene stopped our story. It was a jewel that distracted us. One of the hardest phone calls of my life was trying to explain this to Steve Boles who played Trapp. I don't know if he'll ever forgive me. He can take some solace in the fact that his performance is responsible for a classic song, Steve Earle's "Ellis Unit One." Robert Hilburn of the *Los Angeles Times* wrote that this song, written by Earle after seeing Boles's performance, was the best song written in 1996.

33. Scene 135. We had all been struck by the inhumanity that Helen wrote about in the book of the last moments between mother and son when contact was not allowed. No hugging. We knew this had to be in the movie, so on the day of shooting we let silence sink in at this point and the slightest movement of mother toward son interrupted by the guards. "Can't she hug him?" Prejean says. "I'm sorry Sister, security reasons," responded Beliveau. There was a palpable despair when we were shooting it, and the performances by Susan, Sean, and Roberta Maxwell were absolutely perfect. It was remarkable to see silence carry so much emotion. It was this moment that was cited by a Southern right-wing talk radio host that changed his mind about the death penalty. "I am now against it," he said. "No mother should ever have to go through that."

34. Scene 139. On the day of shooting we switched the order, going instead to scene 142 and 143.

35. Scene 140. Cut from movie. Preceding this scene we shot a scene in the bathroom of Sister Helen alone, asking for God's help, full of fear, seeking strength. It was a great idea proposed by Susan, a moment of desperation amid the mounting tension and pressure in the death house. In the interest of keeping the intensity and oppressiveness of the situation I had the nurse enter the bathroom: the angel of death, intruding on Sister Helen's pleas for strength from God, another violation. This worked incredibly well, and to follow this scene with scene 140 was unnecessary. We needed to get back to Matt.

36. Scene 148. My original intention on the ending of the movie was as follows in this scene. I do believe the film worked with this ending. I loved the scenes outside the prison with the parents. I loved the scene with Helen's mother; it always moved me. The scene in the funeral home was moving and disturbing, and the scene in Hope House with mothers from Helen's community conveying their experiences with violence and the loss of loved ones intercut with the execution worked really well and supplied an interesting texture and irony.

The problem ultimately came down to this. What was the end of the movie? For me it was the small step taken by Delacroix, first in the graveyard and then in the church at the end. It was the slight movement toward reconciliation that left us with hope, with the possibility of love emerging from this madness, this violent world of murder and retributive murder, so everything else, interesting and moving as it was, had to go. Once Matt dies the movie had to move toward its end. It had to get there fast. No one needed to be told what to think or feel at this point in the movie. The emotion was palpable at early screenings. People were devastated. No one needed to be told about Gandhi. No one needed to see Helen's mother or Clyde Percy or anyone else for that matter. Everyone needed resolution, but not forced resolution: an ambiguity, an enigma, a question. One thing I was sure of, when we got to the end I wanted that final shot to last its full length. I didn't want to do any dissolves or shorten the shot in any way. In the ninety seconds or so of that pull back I was hoping for silence, reflection, a simple meditation for all that has transpired. Two people alone in the early morning, an audience thinking of the nature of love, the terror of violence, and the possibility of forgiveness and the redemption it might offer us all.

CAST AND CREW CREDITS

Polygram Filmed Entertainment Presents
A Working Title / Havoc Production
A Film by Tim Robbins

Susan Sarandon   Sean Penn

DEAD MAN WALKING

Robert Prosky	Lois Smith	Margo Martindale
Raymond J. Barry	Scott Wilson	Celia Weston
R. Lee Ermey	Roberta Maxwell	

Casting by
Douglas Aibel

Music by
David Robbins

Costume Design
Renée Ehrlich Kalfus

Production Design
Richard Hoover

Editor
Lisa Zeno Churgin

Director of Photography
Roger A. Deakins, A.S.C.

Executive Producers
Tim Bevan   Eric Fellner

Based on the book
"Dead Man Walking"
by Sister Helen Prejean, C.S. J.

Produced by
Jon Kilik   Tim Robbins
Rudd Simmons

Written and Directed by
Tim Robbins

Sister Helen Prejean	Susan Sarandon	Opossum Kid #2	Gary "Buddy" Boe
Matthew Poncelet	Sean Penn	Opossum Kid #3	Amy Long
Hilton Barber	Robert Prosky	Henry	Dennis F. Neal
Earl Delacroix	Raymond J. Barry	Nellie	Molly Bryant
Clyde Percy	R. Lee Ermey	Mirabeau	Pamela Garmon
Mary Beth Percy	Celia Weston	Reporter	Adrian Colon
Helen's Mother	Lois Smith	Supporter	John D. Wilmot
Chaplain Farley	Scott Wilson	Reporter #1	Margaret Lane
Lucille Poncelet	Roberta Maxwell	Reporter #2	Sally Ann Roberts
Sister Colleen	Margo Martindale	Reporter #3	Alec Gifford
Captain Beliveau	Barton Heyman	Reporter #4	John Hurlbutt
Sgt. Neal Trapp	Steve Boles	News Anchor	Mike Longman
Warden Hartman	Nesbitt Blaisdell	Parent #1	Pete Burris
Luis Montoya	Ray Aranha	Parent #2	Joan Glover
Guy Gilardi	Larry Pine	Parent #3	Florrie Hathorn
Bishop Norwich	Gil Robbins	Parent #4	Lenore Banks
Governor Benedict	Kevin Cooney	Idella	Idella Cassamier
State Trooper	Clancy Brown	Herbie	Marlon Horton
Nurse	Adele Robbins	Kenitra	Kenitra Singleton
Carl Vitello	Michael Cullen	Palmer	Palmer Jackson
Walter Delacroix	Peter Sarsgaard	Johnathan	Johnathan Thomas
Hope Percy	Missy Yager	Guard #1	Walter Breaux, Jr.
Emily Percy	Jenny Krochmal	Guard #2	Scott Sowers
Craig Poncelet	Jack Black	Guard #3	Cortez Nance, Jr.
Sonny Poncelet	Jon Abrahams	Guard #4	Adam Nelson
Troy Poncelet	Arthur Bridgers	Guard #5	Dalvin Ford
Helen's Brother	Steve Carlisle	Guard #6	Derek Steeley
Helen's Sister	Helen Hester	Guard #7	Jeremy Knaster
9-year Old Helen	Eva Amurri	Aide to Governor Benedict	Mary Robbins
Opossum Kid #1	Jack Henry Robbins	Boy in Church	Miles Guthrie Robbins

Donald R. Smith and the Golden Voices Gospel
Choir of St. Francis De Sales Catholic Church

This film is inspired by the events in the life of Sister
Helen Prejean, C.S.J., which she describes in her book
Dead Man Walking. As a dramatization, composite and fic-
tional characters and incidents have been used. Therefore
no inference should be drawn from the events and characters presented here about any of the real persons con-
nected with the life of Sister Helen Prejean, C.S.J.

Unit Production Manager
Rudd Simmons

First Assistant Director
Allan Nicholls

Second Assistant Director
Sam Hoffman

Associate Producer
Allan Nicholls

Production Supervisor
Nancy Kriegel

Sound Mixer	Tod A. Maitland, C.A.S
Film Editor	Ray Hubley
Art Director	Tom Warren
Production Coordinator	Michelle Giordano
Camera Operator	Robin Brown
First Assistant Camera	Andy Harris
Second Assistant Camera	Adam Gilmore
Still Photographer	Demmie Todd
First Assistant Editor	Clare Larson
Second Assistant Editor	Agnès Challe-Grandits
Apprentice Editors	Michael J. Wechsler
	Anne O'Brien
Script Supervisor	Eva Z. Cabrera
Gaffer	Bill O'Leary
Best Boy Electric	William Moore
Second Electric	Jeremy Knaster
Key Grip	Mitch Lillian
Best Boy Grip	Charles Marroquin
Dolly Grip	Bruce Hamme
Boom Operator	T.J. O'Mara
Sound Recordist	Joel Holland
Dialect Coach	Tim Monich
Property Master	Tom Wright
Assistant Property Master	Travis Wright
Key Make-up	Michal Bigger
Ms. Sarandon's Make-up Design	Marilyn Carbone
Key Hair Stylist	Aaron F. Quarles
Mr. Penn's Hair Stylist	Michael Kriston
Assistant Costume Designer	Kim Marie Druce
Wardrobe Supervisors	Hartsell Taylor
	Peter White

Assistant to Tim Robbins	David Carmel
Assistant to the Producers	Shelley Geiler
Assistant to Susan Sarandon	Allison R. Hebble
Assistant to Sean Penn	Holly Cherry
Key Set P.A.	Chris Gilmer
Set P.A.	James Roque, Jr.
Casting Assistant	Jordan Beswick

New York City Unit

Set Decorator	Laurie Friedman
Leadman	Timothy Metzger
Set Dressers	Larry Amanuel
	Harvey Goldberg
	Eric M. Metzger
	Henry Kaplan
Assistant Art Director	David Stein
Art Department Coordinator	Phillis Lehmer
Art Department P.A.	Mary Wigmore
Construction Coordinator	Martin Bernstein
Construction Foreman	Michael Curry, Sr.
Shop Craftsmen	Mark Mann
	Charley Furey
	Richard Kamin
	Eugene J. Hines
Key Construction Grip	Arne Olsen
Construction Grips	Ralph Fratianni
	Kevin A. Tonkin
	Glen Engels
Lead Scenic	James Sorice
Scenics	Margot Therre
	Greg Williams
	Lucian Baran
Scenic Shop Coordinator	Chinyere Ryan
Rigging Gaffer	Richie Ford
Electricians	Greg Addison
	Lance A. Shepherd
	Joe Grimaldi
Rigging Grip	Jonathan Graham
Grips	Gary Martone
	Monique Mitchell
	Tony Arnaud
Additional Hair Stylist	Lizz Scalice
Location Coordinator	Lys Hopper
Stage Manager	Eric David Zoback
Production Accountant	Mindy Sheldon
Asst. Production Accountant	Carla M. Schorr
Accounting Assistants	Melissa Logan
	Joe Lombardi
Asst. Production Coordinators	Peter Schon
	M.J. Magbanua
Production Secretary	Jason Clark Ramsey
Extras Casting	Grant Wilfley
	Vicki Cosentino
Transportation Captain	Louis "Sonny" Volpe

Drivers	John Fitzpatrick
	Peter Aquino
	Ralph Volpe
	James "Dinny" Whalen
DGA Trainee	Patrick Mangan
Camera Trainee	Kris Enos
Set P.A.s	Davis "Flip" Filippi
	Lisa Gaede
Wardrobe P.A.	Alix Hester
Office P.A.s	Jeremy Fader
	Gretchen Hatz
	Michael Remacle
Security P.A.	Greg Cattano
Intern	Nicole Kazdin
Parking Coordinator	Delroy Hunter
Craft Service	Dawn Wolf
	Anthony Monteforte
	Israel Larios
Publicity	Nancy Seltzer & Associates

New Orleans Unit

Art Director	Ken Hardy
Location Manager	Barbara Heller
Assistant Location Managers	Elston Howard
	Dana A. Hanby
Location P.A.	Cynthia Carriere
Second Second Assistant Director	Ann C. Salzer
Set Decorator	Brian S. Kasch
Assistant Set Decorator	Joanne Schmidt
Leadman	Patrick McGuire
On-Set Dresser	Michael Martin
Set Dressers	Jack Blanchard
	E.J. Levron, Jr.
Set Dressing P.A.	Morgan Miller
Art Department Coordinator	Christie Alexander
Art Department P.A.	Shawna Starkman
Construction Coordinator	Nick Rippon
Lead Carpenter	George "Chuck" Stringer, III
Carpenter	John S. Wright
Lead Scenic	Larry Spurlock
Scenics	John Hebert
	Malcolm McClay
Electricians	Mike Smith
	Cougar Easley
	Erskin Mitchell
Grips	Buddy Carr
	Val Zimmer
	Dollar Bill McCord
	Chris Robertson
Property Assistant	Coril Joseph
Second Assistant Camera	Sal Camacho
Assistant Make-up	Allison Gordin
Assistant Hair	Donna Spahn

Additional Wardrobe	Bonney Langfitt
Wardrobe P.A.s	Gina Lombardino
	Jeanne Normand
Asst. Production Coordinator	Sallie Jones Arata
Production Secretary	Bonnie Friedman
Production Accountant	Anne Moosman
Asst. Production Accountant	Kathleen Richter
Set Medic	Susie Blanchard
Local & Extras Casting	Tracy Kilpatrick
Casting Assistant	Rebecca Gibson
Apprentice Editor	Chris Lechler
Editing P.A.	Julie Daggett
Transportation Coordinator	Jerry Everett
Transportation Captain	Al Sens

Drivers

Elven Barrow	Bill Borges
Edward Brumfield	Greg Collins
Charlie Franklin	Huey Grey
Davis Hawn	Jimmy Humphreys
Earl Hurst	Loney Landry
David McMiller	Poland Perkins
Phil Tomalin	Chip Vincent
Bobby Williamson	

Set P.A.s	Scott August
	Christine Donatelli
	Adrian Colon
Office P.A.s	Victoria Person
	Debbie Berins
	Joe Russo
Interns	Nancy Hartman
	Genevieve King
Craft Service	Kayla Chaillot
	Ron Terry
Catering	Location Catering Services
Chefs	Gary Miller
	Brad "Mo" Gremillion
Assistant Chefs	Marcus Barben
	Steven Josephs
Publicity	Katherine Moore & Associates

Post Production Unit

Post Production Supervisor	Graham Stumpf
Sound Editing Services	Hastings Sound Editorial
Supervising Sound Editor	Dan Sable
Re-recording Mixer	Rick Dior
Music Supervisor	David Robbins
Music Editor	Patrick Mullins
Post Production Assistants	Mary Wigmore
	Chris Talbott
Post Prod. Asst. to Tim Robbins	Allison R. Hebble
Post Production Intern	Barry Gastelu
Post Production Accountant	Patrick Sheedy

Sound Editor..Lynn Sable
Dialogue Editors...........Anthony "Chic" Ciccolini, III
                                              Harry Peck Bolles
ADR Editor...Hal Levinsohn
Assistant Sound Editor............................Yvette Nabel
Apprentice Sound Editor.........................Daniel Pagan
Assistant Editor..................................Kristen Johnson
Apprentice Editors.................................Angela Organ
                                                       Sandra Nash
                                                    Eddie Nichols
Editing P.A...................................Shawna Starkman
Recordists...Bob Olari
                                                        Scott Dior
ADR Mixer, New York.............................Paul Zydel
ADR Mixer, Los Angeles...............Charleen Richards
Foley Walker...Bryan Vancho
Foley Mixer ....George Lara

Musicians

Electric and Acoustic Guitars...............David Robbins
Percussion, Wood Flute, Accordion........Mino Cinélu
Uileann Pipes, Bouzouki...........................Seamus Egan
Oud, Kementche, Tambour......................John Vartan
Hammond Organ ....Joel Diamond
Tabla..Dildar Hussain
Harmonium...........................Farrukh Fateh Ali Khan
Drums...David Ratajczak
                                                      Phillip Fisher
Bass Guitars....................................Norwood Fisher
                                                    Frank Centeno
Additional Guitars ....Ry Cooder
                                                    David Spinozza
Violas...Juliet Hafner
                                                         Susan Pray
Violincellos.....................................Eric Friedlander
                                                 Frederick Zlotkin
                                                    Richard Locker
                                                     Eugene Moye
Basses...John Beal
                                                    Ron Wasserman
Vocalists.................................Nusrat Fateh Ali Khan
                                                  Rahat Ali Khan
                                          Farrukh Fateh Ali Khan
                                                    Amina Annabi

The Dusing Singers

Conductor...Gil Robbins
Soloist ....Gale Limansky
Soprano ....Michele Eaton
                                                  Jane Thomgren
                                                   Eileen Reisner
Tenor..Davis Düsing
                                                    Randy Hansen
                                                 Jonathon Pickow

Alto ....Karen Krueger
                                                   Phyllis Jo Kubey
                                                 Elizabeth Norman
                                                     Mary Robbins
Bass ....Kevin Deas
                                                     Wilbur Pauley
                                                    Phillip Snead
Orchestrator ....David Campbell
Choral Arranger ....Gil Robbins
Orchestral Contractor...........................Juliet Haffner
Choral Contractor................................David Düsing
Executive in charge of music for
Polygram Filmed Entertainment ....Dawn Solér
Music Business and Legal Affairs ....Jill Meyer
                                                         Ira Selsky
Music Licensing Manager ....Frankie Pine
Music Project Manager..........................Julianne Kelley
Music Assistant ....David Klotz
New York Music Consultant...............Annie Ohayon
New Orleans Music Consultant ....Alison Miner
Assistant to David Robbins ....Ron James
Score Recorded at National Recording Studios, NYC
Recording Engineer..............................Gary Chester
Assistant Recording Engineer........Yvonne Yedibalian
2nd Asst. Recording Engineer ....Jim Murray
Studio Manager ....Obie O'Brien
Score Mixed at Sony Music Studios, New York
Mixing Engineer .... Gary Chester
Assistant Mixing Engineer.................Robb Williams

Loop Group

Danielle Accarino   Dionna Hickman
Eva Amurri   Aldis Hodge
Lee Arenberg   Edwin Hodge
Ned Bellamy   Tricia Parks
Brian Brophy   Dina Platias
Molly Bryant   Steve Porter
Pierce Cravens   Brian Powell
Abby Fender   Adele Robbins
Jeff Foster   Jack Henry Robbins
Kyle Gass   Dean Robinson
Joe Grimm   Ben Rothman
Hilary Hawkins   Patti Tippo
              Cari Dean Whittemore
Temporary tattoos created by Temptu Studios, NYC
Tattoo Artwork performed by Brad Fox
                                             of Westbank Tattoos
Video Playback ....Brian Carmichael
                                                    Navesync, Inc.
Legal services.............Candice Kersh & Jill Goldstein
                            of Frankfurt, Garbus, Klein & Selz
                                  Howard Fabrick of Proskauer,
                                    Rose, Goetz & Mendelsohn

Legal services (cont.) ....Oliver Goodenough of
Kay Collyer & Boose
Billy Hinshelwood of
Marriot Harrison
Payroll services ....Axium Entertainment Services
Insurance ....RHH/Albert G. Ruben
Insurance Services, Inc.
Completion Guaranty provided by
International Film Guarantors
Lighting Equipment ....Hollywood Rental Co./
Matthews Group
Camera Service Center
Arriflex Cameras and Lenses...Camera Service Center
Dailies Projection...........Boston Light and Sound, Inc.
Laboratory ....DuArt Film Laboratory
Color Timer ....Tom Salvatore
Titles and Opticals ....The Effects House
Pacific Title
Main Titles..............Gary Hawkins of Everett Studios
Digital Film Services...................Pacific Title Digital
Negative Cutting................................J.G.Films, Inc.
Re-recorded at......................................Todd-AO East
Dolby Stereo Consultant................Bradford L. Hohle

For Working Title

Head of Production ....Jane Frazer
Head of Business Affairs..................Angela Morrison
Legal Advisor.....................................Rachel Holroyd
Head of Finance ....Rashid Chinchanwala
President of Development and Production............Liza
Chasin

For Havoc

Associate Producer.....................................Bob White
Associate Producer...................................Mark Seldis

Music

"The Face of Love"
Performed by Nusrat Fateh Ali Khan
with Eddie Vedder
Written by David Robbins, Tim Robbins & Nusrat
Fateh Ali Khan
Nusrat Fateh Ali Khan courtesy of Real World
Records Ltd.
Eddie Vedder courtesy of Epic Records

"This Is the Day the Lord Has Made"
Performed by Rev. Donald R. Smith and
The Golden Voices Gospel Choir of
St. Francis de Sales Catholic Church
Text written by Isaac Watts
Arranged by Donald R. Smith and David Campbell

"A Cool Wind Is Blowing"
Armenian Traditional
Arranged by David Robbins

"Isa Lei"
Performed by Ry Cooder & Vishwa M. Bhatt
Written by A.W. Caten
Courtesy of Water Lily Acoustics, Inc.
& Jhankar Corp.

"Shadow"
Performed and written by Nusrat Fateh Ali Khan
Courtesy of Real World Records Ltd.

"Be Not Afraid"
Performed by Susan Sarandon
Written by Bob Dufford

"In Your Mind"
Performed and written by Johnny Cash
Johnny Cash courtesy of American Recordings

"I Will Not Be Sad in This World"
Armenian Traditional arranged by David Robbins

"Dle Yaman"
Armenian Traditional arranged by David Robbins

"Sacred Love "
Performed by The Dusing Singers
Soloist Gale Limansky
Written by Georgi Sviridov
Arranged by Gil Robbins

"The Long Road"
Performed by Eddie Vedder
With Nusrat Fateh Ali Khan
Written by Eddie Vedder
Eddie Vedder courtesy of Epic Records
Nusrat Fateh Ali Khan
Courtesy of Real World Records Ltd.

"Dead Man Walkin'"
Performed and written by Bruce Springsteen
Bruce Springsteen courtesy of Columbia Records

Selected songs produced by Ry Cooder

"Davey and Goliath—The Easter Special"
Courtesy of The Evangelical Lutheran Church
in America

Special Thanks

Arlene Donovan	Simone Abkarian
Sam Cohn	Clancy Brown
Elaine Goldsmith	Cindy Cook
Bart Walker	Nadine Hasan
	Dr. Katz
Ry Cooder	Erin Kovel
Peter Gabriel	Norik Manoukian
Eddie Vedder	Tom Mikkelsen
The Ali Khan Family	Pliny Porter
Rashid Ahmed Din	Kieran Alexander Presley
Bruce Springsteen	Gabrielle Robbins
Patti Scialfa	Thiery and Chelsea Robbins
Ohayon Media Services, Inc.	Julia Roberts
Real World Records Ltd.	Nicole Vaudry
Michael Kuhn	Suzanne Weinert
Maureen Crowe	Grant Morris
David Daugherty	Sharon Boyle
Deana Elwell	Jack Snyder
Rick Finkelstein	Larry Robinson
Peter Graves	Brigid Boden
Samantha Hart	Jody Silverman
Aline Perry	Ken Hertz
Malcolm Ritchie	Barry Levine
Russell Schwartz	Barry Ancelet
Stewart Till	Marjolaine Sebagh
Mark Wolfe	Jason Barry
Roger Stein	Michael Sartisky

Louisiana Endowment for the Humanities

Steve Castellano and the Staff at Todd-AO East

The Sisters of St. Joseph of Medaille

Sister Lillian Flavin, O.P., Donald Everard
and the Staff of Hope House

Sister Margaret Maggio, C.S.J.

The Residents of the St. Thomas
Housing Development
The St. Thomas Resident Council

The St. Thomas/Irish Channel Consortium

The City of New Orleans, Marc H. Morial, Mayor

New Orleans Film and Video Commission
Kimberly M. Carbo, Director
Elton Jones, Chairman

The City of Covington, Keith Villere, Mayor

The City of Slidell, Sam Caruso, Mayor

The St. Tammany Parish Sheriff's Department

The St. Tammany Parish Tourist and Film Commission
Hyatt Hood, Executive Director

This film was edited on old-fashioned machines.

Music from and inspired by "Dead Man Walking"
Available on Columbia CDs and cassettes

Artists include
Mary Chapin Carpenter
Johnny Cash
Steve Earle
Nusrat Fateh Ali Khan
Lyle Lovett
Michelle Shocked
Patti Smith
Bruce Springsteen
Eddie Vedder
Suzanne Vega
Tom Waits

Read the book: *Dead Man Walking*
by Sister Helen Prejean, C.S.J.
Published by Vintage Books,
a division of Random House, Inc.

The Housing Authority of New Orleans
Michael Kelly, Executive Director

The Louisiana State Penitentiary at Angola
Burl Cain, Warden
R. Dwayne McFatter, Assistant Warden

Malcolm Joseph, New York State Armory
Gayle Carpenter, State of New York,
Division of Military and Naval Affairs

The New York City Mayor's Office for Film,
Theatre and Broadcasting

Filmed on location in Louisiana
and in New York City

The American Humane Association monitored
animal action. Scenes depicting violence to
animals were simulated. No animal was
harmed in the making of this film.

Dedicated to Thelma Bledsoe & Lee Robbins

ABOUT THE AUTHORS

Tim Robbins captured the 1992 Best Actor honors at the Cannes Film Festival and a Golden Globe Award for his work in Robert Altman's *The Player.* The same year, he won critical acclaim in the irreverent satire *Bob Roberts,* his feature directorial debut for which he also wrote the screenplay and the film's musical lyrics. The film played at the director fortnight at Cannes, and won awards at the Belgium, Boston, and Tokyo Film Festivals.

Dead Man Walking has received the Humanities Award, the Christopher Award, the Ecumenical and Audience Prizes at the Berlin Festival, and numerous others. It was also nominated for three Golden Globe Awards and four Academy Awards®, winning the Best Actress Oscar for Susan Sarandon.

As an actor Robbins has also created memorable characters in films such as *The Shawshank Redemption, Short Cuts, Jacob's Ladder, Bull Durham,* and *Five Corners,* among others.

Helen Prejean, C.S.J., is a writer, lecturer, and community organizer who has lived and worked in Louisiana all her life. She has lectured extensively on the subject of capital punishment and has appeared on *ABC World News Tonight, 60 Minutes,* BBC World Service radio, and an NBC special series on the death penalty. She has written articles for numerous publications including the *San Francisco Chronicle* and the *Baltimore Sun.* She is a member of the Sisters of St. Joseph of Medaille.

In 1982, Prejean became the spiritual advisor to Patrick Sonnier, the convicted killer of two teenagers who was sentenced to die in the electric chair in Louisiana's State Penitentiary at Angola. Out of that relationship came her book *Dead Man Walking,* a profoundly moving spiritual journey through America's system of capital punishment.